DEVELOPING SUCCESSFUL
SPORT MARKETING PLANS

Titles in the
Sport Management Library

— • —

Case Studies in Sport Marketing

— • —

Developing Successful Sport Marketing Plans, 3rd Edition

— • —

Developing Successful Sport Sponsorship Plans, 3rd Edition

— • —

Economics of Sport, 2nd Edition

— • —

Ethics & Morality in Sport Management

— • —

Financing Sport, 2nd Edition

— • —

Foundations of Sport Management

— • —

Fundamentals of Sport Marketing, 3rd Edition

— • —

Media Relations in Sport, 2nd Edition

— • —

Sport Facility Management: Organizing Events and Mitigating Risks

— • —

Sport Governance in the Global Community

— • —

Sport Management Field Experiences

DEVELOPING SUCCESSFUL SPORT MARKETING PLANS

THIRD EDITION

David K. Stotlar, EdD

UNIVERSITY OF NORTHERN COLORADO

Fitness Information Technology
A Division of the International Center
for Performance Excellence
262 Coliseum, WVU-PASS, PO Box 6116
Morgantown, WV 26506-6116

Library of Congress Card Catalog Number: 2008928087

ISBN 13: 978-1-885693-84-6

Production Editor: Matt Brann
Cover Design: Craig Hines
Typesetter: Craig Hines
Copyeditor: Danielle Costello
Proofreader: Erica Reib
Indexer: Matt Brann
Printed by Data Reproductions Corporation
Cover photo courtesy of Keith Syvinski/Stock.xchng

10 9 8 7 6 5 4 3 2

Fitness Information Technology
A Division of the International Center for Performance Excellence
West Virginia University
262 Coliseum, WVU-PASS
PO Box 6116
Morgantown, WV 26506-6116
800.477.4348 (toll free)
304.293.6888 (phone)
304.293.6658 (fax)
Email: fitcustomerservice@mail.wvu.edu
Website: www.fitinfotech.com

Table of Contents

Detailed Table of Contents

Preface

The third edition of *Developing Successful Sport Marketing Plans* was developed to serve as a companion to *Fundamentals of Sport Marketing*, 3rd Ed. (Pitts & Stotlar, 2007). Changes have been made from the second edition of this workbook, directing the focus on the sport consumer rather than the product, reflecting the dynamics in the industry. The book draws on the author's experience in academia and as a sport marketing consultant. Although a more thorough review of sport marketing theory is presented in *Fundamentals of Sport Marketing*, this text provides an overview of the theoretical fundamentals of the topic, supported by specific examples from actual sport organizations. In some cases, the name of the sport organization has been changed for reasons of confidentiality. Most chapters also provide worksheets for constructing a custom marketing plan for the reader's own sport organization.

The intent is simple: Provide a workbook to assist the reader in creating a marketing plan through a well-defined, industry-proven protocol. This workbook provides a sequential process for building a winning marketing plan that has proven to be successful.

Acknowledgments

I first want to recognize the support and understanding of my wife and life partner, Sylvia. Without her sense of humor and challenging my naïve comments, the book would be less interesting. I also want to thank all the students and colleagues who, over the years, have been willing to tell me exactly what they think about the book. Many students working in the industry often call and say they are using what they learned and have kept the books as a guide. This is the ultimate compliment—that the material is usable and pertinent to succeeding in the industry.

I also want to thank the publisher and editors at Fitness Information Technology for their patience and persistence in the development and publication of this edition. I look forward to many future editions.

David K. Stotlar

Chapter One

DEVELOPING A MARKETING FRAMEWORK

Introduction

Sport, in the United States, is a $410 billion industry (Plunkett Research, 2007), ranking it among America's largest. Meek (1997, p. 16) developed the term *gross domestic sports product* (GDSP) to capture both the breadth and depth of the industry. Details of the industry are presented below. An almost doubling of the industry in the last 5 years ($213–$410 billion) speaks to the significant and rapid growth of the industry. It should be noted, however, that precise calculation of the economic activity within any one industrial sector is difficult (Meek, 1997; King 2002; Pitts & Stotlar, 2007). Before values can be assigned, one must define which segments make up the industry and just what should be included in each segment.

Table 1.1. Sport Industry Categories

Rank	Category	Size
1	Sport Advertising	$27.43 billion
2	Spectator Spending	$26.17 billion
3	Sporting Goods	$25.62 billion
4	Team/League Operating Expenses	$22.98 billion
5	Sport Gambling	$18.90 billion
6	Sport Travel	$16.06 billion
7	Professional Services	$15.25 billion
8	Sport Medicine	$12.60 billion
9	Licensed Sporting Goods	$10.50 billion
10	Media Broadcast Rights	$6.99 billion
11	Sport Sponsorships	$6.40 billion
12	Sports Facility Construction	$2.48 billion
13	Sport Multimedia	$2.12 billion
14	Endorsements	$897.00 million
15	Internet Spending	$239.10 million

(Information adopted from King, 2002)

Pitts and Stotlar (2007) indicated that an *industry* comprises a wide variety of related products that are sold to consumers. In most industries, there is an assortment of products types and a significant variance in the consumer base. Therefore, as Pitts and Stotlar (2007) indicated, the best assessment of an industry is to examine the various segments that represent the products and services offered to consumers.

Sport is a collective noun that includes all activities meeting the criteria of active participation. It differs from the term *sports*, which implies a collection of physical activities. Thus, the sport industry encompasses a vast array of commercial endeavors surrounding specific sports. In Pitts, Fielding, and Miller's (1994) seminal work, they segmented the sport industry into *sport performance*, *sport production*, and *sport promotion*. The *sport performance* segment would include all elements related to sport participation and spectating, such as professional and amateur sport, sport education, membership-based sport organizations, and not-for-profit sport programs (municipal sport).

The *sport production* segment of the industry would include those products needed for the production of sport performance. Some of the elements comprising this segment are sport equipment and apparel, as well as services that enhance performance (fitness trainers, medical care, sport therapy, and sport governing bodies). It is a significant sector: Americans spent more than $60 billion on sports apparel and footwear in 2006 (SGMA, 2006). The last segment contains products and services related to promoting sport. Sport media, merchandising, sport sponsorship, and athlete endorsements are all examples of economic activity that would fall into this category.

Meek (1997) segmented the industry into sport entertainment, sport products, and sport support organizations. While these differ somewhat from Pitts et al., both incorporate all of the major contributors to the economic activity associated with sport. Meek expressed concern about attempts to measure the economic components of the industry. His most important point is that "one cannot 'double-count,' or account for the same dollars two or more ways" (p. 16). Furthermore, Meek believes most estimates of the GDSP mistakenly count spending accounted for elsewhere in the economy. For instance, he specifies that player salaries and endorsement dollars must not be included in the GDSP because they are ultimately reflected in the GDSP through the price consumers pay at retail.

Thus, discussion of the calculated value of the sport industry depends on decisions relating to which economic sectors spending should be assigned. Data indicate that only 20% of people use sports clothing for sport participation, so a question arises whether those expenditures should be included in the GDSP or in the footwear and fashion industry. Is the money spent in travel for a golf trip attributable to the sport industry or the travel industry? Sport advertising in newspapers, magazines, and in stadiums demonstrated considerable value, yet Meek indicates they are not part of the GDSP. In conclusion, Meek stated, "in estimating the size of the industry, final consumption is really all that matters" (p. 17).

| **Marketing** Defined | Kotler and Armstrong (2006) interpret marketing as utilization of a company's resources for the purpose of meeting consumer wants and needs. They further elaborated on the importance of marketing by stating that "marketing is a social and managerial process by which individuals and groups obtain what they need and want through creating and exchanging value with others. Hence, we define marketing as the process by which companies create value for customers and build strong customer relationships in order to capture value from customers in return" (p. 5). These thoughts can be more narrowly applied to specific industries, such as sport. |

| ***Sport Marketing* Defined** | Pitts and Stotlar (2007, p. 69) defined sport marketing as "the process of designing and implementing activities for the production, pricing, promotion, and distribution of a sport or sport business product to satisfy the needs or desires of consumers and to achieve the company's objectives." Thus, the focus of sport marketing falls jointly on the consumers and the company. Yet, priority must be given to meeting consumers' needs. Ultimately this must be the overall focus of the company. As Farris, Bendle, Pfeifer, and Reibstein (2006, p. 45) noted, "The purpose of a business is to create a customer." While there are many in sport management who focus on organizational behavior, sport finance, and other worthy topics, it remains clear . . . if you do not have customers, there is no need for the company. |

Historically, corporations have been designed to manufacture products and sell them to consumers. Early in the formulation of marketing as a concept, many managers saw marketing as synonymous with selling. However, during the 1960s, a more advanced concept of marketing began to take shape. Mullin, Hardy, and Sutton (2007) discussed this shift in the marketing concept. The traditional concept is product oriented—sell what you make. The new, more modern, idea is customer or market oriented—make what will sell. This concept focuses on the notion that marketing is the key to securing and satisfying customers. A marketing myopia results if you "focus on producing and selling goods and services rather than identifying and satisfying the needs and wants of customers" (Mullin, Hardy, & Sutton, 2007, p. 12).

In a free market economy, consumers have a variety of choices. As a result of customer choice, an estimated 90% of new businesses are unsuccessful (Pride & Ferrell, 2008). The institutions that survive are most likely to be those most adept at meeting the needs and wants of consumers. To accomplish that, you need a well-defined marketing plan. As noted earlier, sport is a multibillion-dollar industry, yet it is amazing how many sport organizations do not have marketing plans for their products and services.

| **Marketing Framework** | Marketing plans serve several critical roles within the organization. Cohen (1998, p. 3) commented that a marketing plan "allows everyone to see how their actions fit in with the actions of others." Furthermore, Cohen (1998) and McDonald and Keegan (2003) suggest that marketing plans can |

- provide a road map for corporate development,
- assist in the management and implementation of strategy,

- communicate role specificity to new employees,
- coordinate the assignment of responsibilities and tasks,
- assist in obtaining resources for development,
- promote efficient use of resources (people, facilities, and finances),
- identify sources of competitive advantage, and
- point out problems, opportunities, and threats.

Within the sport industry, many executives think of a marketing plan as a corporate "game plan." For readers with sport participation or coaching experience, this analogy should prove beneficial throughout this workbook.

Considerable debate exists on what should come first, the creation of a value proposition (the product or service) or a study of the marketing environment. Marketing theory leads with a study of the market. This market-first orientation is the most contemporary, and it will serve those who have an existing product or service in the market. However, the author's experience has shown that many sport entrepreneurs start with a product or service idea and then find markets that are appropriate for their offering, eventually customizing the offering based on the targeted consumers. Thus, the structure of this book will start with the value proposition.

PLANNING

The initial step in creating a marketing plan involves a considerable amount of planning. While this may seem obvious, lack of planning plagues many sport organizations. Hiebing and Cooper (2003, p. 1) noted, "The key to writing a good marketing plan is disciplined marketing planning." All too often, organizations get so involved in tackling their day-to-day management tasks, and they tend to subordinate planning. The impediments to planning are that planning takes time and planning takes coordination (Stevens, Loudon, Wrenn, & Warren, 1997). Time is one of the most precious commodities within most sport organizations, and coordination necessitates getting the organization's top executives together, at one time, to focus on one issue. When that issue is the future success of the enterprise, its importance cannot be minimized. Stevens et al. (1997, p. 13) noted, "Nowhere in the organization is planning more needed than in marketing. The complexity of today's environment in terms of social, legal, environmental, economic, competitive, and resource constraints requires a high degree of skill to provide structure to a course of action an organization can follow to achieve desired results."

ORGANIZING TO PLAN

Depending on the size and complexity of an organization, the team required to develop the marketing plan varies. In large and complex sport organizations, marketing plans are typically initiated in strategic business units (SBUs) and then forward to top-level executives for inclusion in the overall corporate marketing plan. For example, at Reebok (now a part of the adidas group), one of their SBUs, Reebok Running, developed marketing strategies within the unit, yet in consort with Reebok and adidas Group top management. In smaller organizations, the chief executive officer (CEO) will most likely be intimately involved in creating and guiding the marketing plan. Illustrations of this concept are seen in many national governing bodies for United States amateur sport. With taekwondo appearing as a medal sport for the first time at the 2000 Sydney Olympic Games, the U.S. Taekwondo Union completed a marketing plan to more thoroughly prepare for its future. Regardless of the plan selected, getting organized is a start in the right direction.

COMPONENTS OF THE MARKETING FRAMEWORK

The *executive summary* is the last part of the plan written, but the first one encountered by a reader. Kotler and Armstrong (2006) suggest that an executive summary should provide the reader with a concise review of the entire plan. This also allows potential investors to quickly assess if the enterprise is worthy of consideration. If such a decision is favorable, a reader will continue examining the entire marketing plan. Thus, a significant amount of importance rides on the executive summary. The challenge lies in producing a compelling and succinct summary.

At a minimum, the items that should be covered in your executive summary are

- an accurate and specific description of your product or service,
- a description of the advantages of your product or service,
- an overview of the finances involved, and
- projected profit or return on investment.

Depending on the length of the marketing plan, a table of contents should probably follow the executive summary to direct readers through the remainder of the document.

As proposed by Cohen (1998), the remaining content of the marketing plan should include the components discussed below.

Introduction

The introduction typically begins with the organization's mission statement, which represents the purpose of the organization. In general terms, the statement should reflect the essence of your business by answering the question, "What business are you in?"

Creating a Value Proposition (Chapter 2)

Kotler and Armstrong (2006) defined the *value proposition* as the set of benefits created to satisfy consumer needs. This includes clarification of the products or services offered, also called the *marketing offer*. A thorough product and service analysis, as well as the market position, should be clearly developed in the plan. The writer will want to discuss the unique characteristics of the organization's product/service, addressing its fit in the marketplace.

Understanding the Market Environment (Chapter 3)

This section of the marketing plan is intended to provide an analysis of the environment in which the organization must operate. Cohen (1998) suggests that this section might also be called "environmental scanning" (p. 10). This process is critical for successful planning, and thus, subsequent sections should address this process. In general, the factors that shape the situational analysis include a review of the following: the economic climate, population demographics, product demand trends, industrial technological trends, competitor analysis, and the internal aspects of the organization related to management and employees.

Target Markets (Chapter 4)

The target market segment of the marketing plan provides for a description of the consumer base. This entails a detailed analysis of the customers who are most likely to buy the organization's product. Typically, this analysis consists of information related to the purchasing habits of the customers, as well as data on the characteristics of consumers—such as age, gender, lifestyle, and income. These consumer characteristics are used to segment the market, allowing for more direct access and further analysis.

With the proliferation of computer technology, many organizations will create a database to manage this task. This database has also been called a *marketing information system*. Specific steps in the creation of marketing information systems are provided in Chapter 4.

Marketing Objectives (Chapter 5)

All organizations need to have clearly established objectives to guide their actions. This is, therefore, a critical aspect of a marketing plan. The old saying, "If you don't know where you are going, any road will get you there" should provide an understandable rationale for setting marketing objectives. Chapter 5 of this workbook provides more information to assist in the creation of marketing objectives. However, most marketing authorities suggest that a marketing plan should include statements related to an organization's projected market share, sales volume, profit margins, and product positioning (Kotler & Armstrong, 2006; Cohen, 1998; Hiebing & Cooper, 2003; Stevens, Loudon, Wrenn, & Warren, 1997).

Marketing Strategies and Tactics (Chapters 6 and 7)

Some marketing scholars separate marketing strategies from marketing tactics. Marketing strategies (Chapter 6) normally refer to *what* marketing activities an organization plans to undertake, whereas marketing tactics relate to *how* the organization will accomplish those objectives. However, in most organizations the two components are often tied together in marketing discussions. The suggestion here is that, while a marketing plan may engage in discussions that tie the two concepts together, they should eventually be separated. For example, a marketer may develop a great idea about what to do, but problems may arise when implementation is considered. There may also be several methods to accomplish the same action. Separating the concepts allows for more creative solutions.

There has been some discussion in the literature regarding whether the *marketing mix*, a traditional ingredient of marketing, exists as a marketing strategy or as a tactic. Cohen (1998, p. 13) indicates that marketing mix variables are "really tactical because they are actions taken to accomplish the strategy you develop." Therefore, the marketing mix (price, product, place, promotion) is presented separately in this workbook in Chapter 7. Through the manipulation of these elements, several variations of strategy can arise. These can be categorized into market actions known as penetration, diversification, new product development, market share expansion, and niche development, among others.

Implementation, Control, and Evaluation (Chapter 8)

This chapter of the marketing plan should contain information needed for start-up and operational costs, public relations, cost analyses methods, and general budget parameters. In addition, managers must be cognizant of the progress made on the accomplishment of the stated objectives. In this matter, criteria and processes must be established for monitoring your progress. As with all organizations, periodic measures must be made in relation to organizational performance.

Finally, a brief passage should be provided to summarize the preceding chapters of the marketing plan. The summary should bring the reader back to the mission of the organization and how that mission will be activated through the actions, strategies, and tactics outlined in the plan.

Marketing Ethics

Pride and Ferrell (2008) indicated that the parameters of marketing ethics begin with the laws regulating commerce and expand to include decisions regarding the interaction between personal values and business demands. The primary issue with ethical behavior is that oftentimes the decision as to whether the action is "right" or "wrong" is not easily discernible.

In today's competitive market, success in sales often comes at the expense of ethical decision making. For example, exaggerated claims are often made for the performance characteristics of sport products. While often backed up by data, that data may be of limited scientific merit or may have been conducted through grants provided to the research firm, suggesting a potential conflict of interest for the researchers. Advertising in recent years has featured carefully worded comparisons to competitors' products. Many marketing campaigns thrive on carefully crafted "truths." At times, marketing managers may be pushed to rush a product to market, even before safety testing is complete. In these cases, some corporations decide that it will be cheaper to pay out-of-court settlements for incurred injuries than to halt manufacturing and product design.

Other examples and ethical dilemmas arise that test sport marketers. A scheduled promotion with the Los Angeles "Laker Girls" may be successful in filling an arena, but you must decide if the organization condones what many believe to be the exploitation of women as sex objects. The violence in ice hockey could certainly be used in marketing campaigns to sell more tickets; however, promoting violence may not be the most ethical marketing strategy.

Much of the responsibility for marketing ethics lies in the hands of upper management. If marketing or sales people who behave in what most would consider an unethical manner are rewarded or not punished, others may believe that this behavior is acceptable. "Most experts agree that the chief executive officer or vice president of marketing sets the ethical tone for the entire marketing organization" (Pride & Ferrell, 2008, p. 99).

BEST PRACTICE

Outline of a Fictitious Marketing Plan for Rocky Mountain Sports Academy

1. EXECUTIVE SUMMARY

Rocky Mountain Sports Academy (RMSA) provides the community with a complete youth sports program for participants from kindergarten to high school through positive learning and team experiences. RMSA is the area's leading provider of youth sports experiences and seeks to make this experience affordable and available for all members of the community. Rocky Mountain Sports Academy now serves more than 24,000 participants in seven sports throughout the area.

Rocky Mountain Sports Academy possesses a commanding percentage of the total market share. This is based on the estimated number of participants compared to participation levels in other programs, both public and private. This share percentage drops in high school due to increased competition from other organizations as well as in-school programs offered through the public school system.

Specific goals of the marketing plan:

1. Expand into new areas within Weld County that desire access to Rocky Mountain Sports Academy activities.
2. Leverage the growth offered by the increasing interest in soccer in the fall and spring programs.
3. Identify additional facilities to support future growth and offer greater flexibility in scheduling.
4. Continue to develop corporate contributions that add to the financial resources of the participant fees.

2. INTRODUCTION

Started in 1988, Rocky Mountain Sports Academy (RMSA) provides sport and athletic programming to the youth of Northern Colorado. The Mission of RMSA is to provide all youth with the highest quality education and team experience through sports participation. Participants are treated with respect through the opportunity to experience growth in the areas of teamwork, sportsmanship, fair play, skill development, and interacting with others. The goal is to create a positive environment that fosters improved self-confidence and self-esteem through experiences in sports activities.

3. VALUE PROPOSITION

The "Rocky Mountain Sports Academy experience" is designed to offer the following to each participant:

• Recreation through participation in organized team sports.

- The opportunity to learn and experience a variety of sports.
- A means to improve athletic skills.
- A means to learn teamwork, sportsmanship, and fair play.
- A source of fun and enjoyment to enrich their lives.
- An opportunity to enhance their health and fitness.

The parents and guardians of the participants also realize benefits. They are able to offer their children a positive, well-supervised experience as they learn the skills described above that does not necessarily require the parents' time.

4. SITUATION ANALYSIS

In recent years, school-sponsored sports programs have been significantly reduced, severely limiting the number and range of sport activities offered. Based on a recent study, 59% of the people in the Weld County area surveyed believe the public school system fails to meet their sports experience expectations. Driven by economics, most notably with the passage of state legislation limiting school funding, many sports programs have not survived increasing economic pressures on the public school system.

The need for youth sports programs is validated and magnified by information that attributes long-term value to participants in these programs. Numerous studies document the direct value of youth participation in sports. These studies indicate a direct correlation demonstrating that involvement in sports results in reducing the potential to become involved in drugs, sex, crime, and gang-related behaviors. Research indicates the economic, social, and personal value of "investing" in the lives of children in a positive and constructive manner avoids the social and penal system costs that may later result. To meet this need, Rocky Mountain Sports Academy offers an experience that serves as a personal "sports reference" for participants throughout their lives. These important benefits continue to validate the Rocky Mountain Sports Academy concept.

Table 1.2. Market Analysis

Potential Customers	2006	2007	2008	2009	2010	Growth
Public School Students	1,947	2,064	2,188	2,319	2,458	6.00%
Private School Students	388	423	461	502	547	8.97%
Home School Students	107	125	146	171	200	16.93%
Total	2,442	2,612	2,795	2,992	3,205	7.03%

Competitor Analysis

A number of other programs offer youth sports experiences. None of these programs offer the extensive range of experiences or infrastructure of Rocky Mountain Sports Academy. Some programs do, however, offer specific attributes some participants and parents find attractive. This is particularly true for those who seek a higher level of competition and competitive screening of participants.

Direct competitors to Rocky Mountain Sports Academy include:

- Babe Ruth Baseball/American Legion Baseball
- No. Colo. Volleyball
- City of Greeley Basketball
- ASA Softball
- Colorado Youth Soccer
- AYSO Soccer
- Theo's Gymnastics Academy

Table 1.3. Price Comparison

Competitor	Average Program Price
Rocky Mountain Sports Academy	$85
Babe Ruth Baseball	$120
No. Colorado Volleyball	$150
City of Greeley Basketball	$90
ASA Softball	$95
Colorado Youth Soccer	$110
AYSO Soccer	$105
Theo's Gymnastics Academy	$135

SWOT Analysis

Strengths

Program Reputation—Rocky Mountain Sports Academy is considered to be the premier choice for youth sports related experiences. There is now a generation of participants that send their children to participate in the program.

Sponsorship Base—We have developed a stable and loyal sponsor base from both private and corporate sources.

Facilities Relationships—We depend on access to athletic facilities including gyms, soccer fields, football fields, softball, and baseball fields. Close relationships and reciprocal maintenance agreements with public and private schools and church facilities are an invaluable asset to the organization.

The Internet—Our website, http://www.RockyMountainSportsAcademy.com, promises to be a significant technological solution for Rocky Mountain Sports Academy in the area of registration, communication, and information delivery. The website has demonstrated the ability to provide more extensive and current information at reduced costs. We can reduce the need for printed materials, voicemail communication equipment, and staff payroll time.

Weaknesses

Capital Requirements—Rocky Mountain Sports Academy continues to make impressive improvements in the management of financial resources. Additional funds are needed to maintain the quality of the experiences offered and to meet future program demands. The Fundraising Foundation's strategy is to provide significant financial resources for Rocky Mountain Sports Academy. The future depends on these resources, in addition to revenues from participants and traditional fundraising events.

Facilities—Our need for facilities is growing beyond what is now available. This is one of the most urgent challenges facing Rocky Mountain Sports Academy. This essential component is threatened by increasing program needs, combined with recent restrictions and fees for the use of public school facilities. Indoor facilities are virtually at capacity for basketball and volleyball games and tournaments. They are insufficient to support flexible and convenient practice schedules. Outdoor facilities are adequate, but the increasing demands of soccer present a concern in this area as well. New and innovative alternatives must be explored and implemented to provide additional facilities to support the demands of the program. One alternative is to form alliances with public facilities to take on the management and maintenance of these facilities in exchange for scheduled use. Other potential options may include constructing wholly-owned facilities for the Academy.

Training and Education for Coaches and Officials—Individuals often have their first coaching experience with Rocky Mountain Sports Academy. This presents the need to adequately train these individuals to enable them to better understand Rocky Mountain Sports Academy's philosophy, their responsibilities, potential liability issues, and appropriate behavior with participants. A more positive experience for participants, coaches, and officials and an increased awareness of responsibilities are some of the goals. The resource demands of this training effort are tremendous.

Staff Challenges and Attrition—The Rocky Mountain Sports Academy's staff experiences tremendous pressure due to workloads, dealing with parents, and addressing the issues of the program. These factors, combined with concerns regarding compensation, have resulted in undesirable turnover in important positions.

Opportunities

Rocky Mountain Sports Academy competes for participants in a community with a high number of options. Based on this challenge, Rocky Mountain Sports Academy must continue to demonstrate that it successfully offers a meaningful experience to participants, with short and long-term benefits, in a manner that effectively meets consumer needs. The following summarizes potential opportunities:

Geographic Service Area—Rocky Mountain Sports Academy continues to be a precedent-setting organization that attracts attention from surrounding communities. Decisions regarding the service area will impact financial requirements and potentially open new revenue opportunities. This growth strategy must be managed and orchestrated in a manner that will add strength to the program.

Soccer Interest—Soccer is the single fastest growing sport in terms of participation (based principally on the growth in the Hispanic population). With some participation decrease in boy's football, this increasing interest in soccer is the most predominant reason for program growth and has added a more even balance to gender participation. There is an increasing demand for indoor soccer programs.

Program Expansion—Program expansion also requires consideration and evaluation. This may include adding sports such as lacrosse to the current menu or looking at offering sports to older age groups, potentially including adult sports programs.

Community Education—Rocky Mountain Sports Academy must continue to tell its story to the community it serves. This message is one that reinforces the philosophy and the purpose for its existence. A well-informed community may effectively ensure public facilities are available for use based on reasonable expectations placed on Rocky Mountain Sports Academy.

Threats

Philosophy Changes—The willingness of the public school and other partners to provide their facilities for use by Rocky Mountain Sports Academy. The precise ramifications of this situation are not known, but all potential outcomes must be considered as plans are made for the coming years.

Alternative Programs—The increasing impact from other programs, ranging from organization-sponsored to club sports, poses a threat to a segment of Rocky Mountain Sports Academy's market. These organizations target the highly skilled and committed players and coaches and are eroding the depth and breadth of Rocky Mountain Sports Academy's participant and coach resources.

Legal and Liability Issues—Rocky Mountain Sports Academy continues to be exposed to liability issues in many aspects of the experience it provides. The potential concerns range from health and safety issues to various forms of verbal or physical abuse. In an increasingly litigious society, there is always potential for legal action.

The "Elite/Advanced" Sports Dilemma—Providing competitive environments for athletes with higher skill levels who seek to be in an intentionally competitive arena is in question. The threat of not offering this option is that these athletes may be drawn away from Rocky Mountain Sports Academy by alternative programs. Some of the most highly trained and experienced coaches can also be attracted to these other programs. This issue challenges some of Rocky Mountain Sports Academy's most basic philosophies.

5. ANALYSIS OF TARGET MARKETS

Rocky Mountain Sports Academy offers a unique experience for children that want to have an enjoyable sports experience. All youth between the ages of 5 and 18 can participate in one or more sports throughout the year. Their participation is not dependent upon their previous experience, skill level, or athletic ability. Everyone can play. The breadth, depth, and overall quality of the sports experience we offer cannot be matched within our market. Based on significant demographic changes and the expanding Hispanic population (a lager portion of which is at the lower end of the economic spectrum), cost containment will be a primary objective. We work with parents and guardians to add to their child's sports experiences. Rocky Mountain Sports Academy exists to create a cherished childhood memory for each participant.

Rocky Mountain Sports Academy provides valuable team and social experiences for the increasing population of public, private, and home-schooled youth. RMSA offers young people the opportunity to participate in a variety of team sports throughout the calendar year. Beginning in kindergarten, these experiences provide a source of recreation and simultaneously improve athletic skills, health, and fitness as they offer experiences in teamwork, sportsmanship, fair play, cooperation, and leadership. Increased self confidence is just one of the many intangible benefits this program offers.

6. MARKETING OBJECTIVES

The objective is to provide this valuable experience to as many children as possible in a positive and supportive manner. A positive, constructive, and meaningful experience is the sought-after result of the Rocky Mountain Sports Academy experience. This experience may assist individuals to better understand the necessary skills that life demands and empower them to realize the choices and options available to them.

1. Increase participation 15% to 27,500 through the current fiscal year.
2. Accomplish program goals within the budget of $1,510,000.
3. Increase return on investor capital by 3%.
4. Expand the program to two new schools within our serving area by August, prior to the next academic year.
5. Maintain market share advantages over competitors.

7. MARKETING STRATEGIES

Rocky Mountain Sports Academy is a for-profit organization and must continue to devote a portion of the budget to promotion to continue to ensure broad participation and return on investor capital. Strong participation ensures that Rocky Mountain Sports Academy can meet stated revenue objectives. Strong participation also means that Rocky Mountain Sports Academy offers sporting programs to all skill levels across a broad spectrum of programs, ensuring that anyone who wants to participate can participate.

The Rocky Mountain Sports Academy marketing mix consists of a pricing strategy that fosters participation while adequately funding operations and a promotion strategy that ensures continued participation in our programs. Rocky Mountain Sports Academy strives to be the premier provider of sports experiences for children in the areas served. Programs are in place to simultaneously serve the needs of out-of-district participants in a manner that is positive for these participants and enhances revenue streams for Rocky Mountain Sports Academy with minimal additional costs.

The goal of the marketing strategy is to effectively represent the unique value of the program to potential participants. A particular focus will be directed on the many benefits of involvement in the program, rather than associated costs. The marketing strategy will continue to identify the needs of the market and communicate with this audience in the most compelling and positive manner possible.

Ongoing efforts continually attempt to understand how Rocky Mountain Sports Academy can maintain the quality and integrity of the program within the finite financial resources of participants and the community of donors and supporters. This challenge is increasing. As costs continue to increase in a number of areas, the demands and expectations of the participants and their parents do as well. Rocky Mountain Sports Academy is constantly working to improve the program through improvements and changes in its structure and implementation. Quality and efficiency are just two goals of these changes.

The marketing strategies of market penetration (maintenance of market share), market expansion (adding adult programming), and new product development (adding new sports) will be pursued based on continued attention to the quality of the experience, in conjunction with identifying opportunities to expand the participation of the programs where possible.

8. IMPLEMENTATION AND CONTROL

The purpose of the Rocky Mountain Sports Academy marketing plan is to serve as a guide to the staff and the Board of Directors to continue to improve the organization and its ability to serve the youth of Weld County. We must successfully activate the marketing plan to accomplish our goals. Failing to implement even one of the programs could be devastating to our success. Rocky Mountain Sports Academy will have weekly "milestones" meetings to review current milestone status, funding status, and status of the actual programs. For Rocky Mountain Sports Academy, it is critical to maintain consistent focus on implementation, not only in order to maintain strong programs, but to maintain strong relationships with participants and other funding sources. A specific implementation calendar provides the milestones to assure the attainment of the objectives and overall program quality.

Chapter Two

CREATING A VALUE PROPOSITION

Value Propositions and Marketing Offers

One of the contemporary concepts that shape the marketing environment is *value proposition*, the set of benefits created to satisfy consumer needs. The value proposition signifies what it is that you promise to deliver to the customer, regardless of whether it is classified and a product or a service. It could even be a feeling or memorable experience. Therefore, sport marketers typically package benefits in the value proposition across many variables through a customized "marketing offer." Kotler and Armstrong (2006, p. 6) defined a marketing offer as a "combination of products, services, information and experiences offered to a market to satisfy a need or want." Pitts and Stotlar (2007) provide a complete overview of this issue in *Fundamentals of Sport Marketing*.

Defining Products and Services

The word *product* must become an integral part of the sport marketer's vocabulary. Many marketers use the term to describe both the output of specific manufactured goods and the programs and services provided. Thus, services are products and can be part of a product. Perhaps a term that better describes products and services in a sport environment is *product offerings*.

Product offerings may be clearly distinguishable as either a product or service, yet many in the sport industry provide both components concurrently. Pitts and Stotlar (2007) define product to include goods, services, people, places, and ideas. For example, a fitness center provides the services of an aerobic instructor for an exercise class. That same business also sells aerobic apparel and shoes in its on-site pro shop. This is also true of college and university athletic programs that offer sporting events for spectators, as well as novelties and souvenirs. Sports events do not clearly fall into the category of either a product or a service. Mullin, Hardy, and Sutton (2007) indicate that sport has several unique elements that differentiate it from other business products marketed in the general economy. They point out that the sporting event is perishable, that it has no shelf life. This means that if it is not sold or used, it is lost. If a consumer is interested in obtaining tickets to a particular game or event and went to the stadium to purchase a ticket, they would probably find numerous people outside of the gates with tickets for sale. Depending on the scarcity of tickets for that game, the prices would certainly vary. However, ten minutes after the start of the contest, the price may begin to decline, and one hour after the start, the tickets may, in fact, be worthless. This differs considerably from hard goods. If they are not sold today, there is always tomorrow. Pitts and Stotlar (2007) place sports events into the sport performance segment of the industry.

Mullin, Hardy, and Sutton (2007) point out that sport marketers have little control over the product. In industry, a product may not sell well because of its color or style. A marketer would certainly discuss this with the production division so that changes could be made to offer consumers a product more to their liking. In professional or collegiate sport, the marketer cannot go to a coach and demand that the style of play be changed in order to make it easier to sell tickets. The sporting goods industry is of course able to respond to these concerns, but for much of the sport industry, the stated challenge applies. According to the Oakland A's vice president of marketing, "We're in an industry that has almost no control over its product" (Salerno, 1991, p. 44).

The sport industry is often more involved with services than with manufactured goods (over 60% of the nation's GDP is in the service sector). Professional and amateur sports teams, health and fitness centers, stadiums, arenas, and country clubs are all involved primarily with the provision of sport-related services. Sporting goods manufacturers, along with their wholesalers and retailers, are in the business of producing and supplying consumer goods. Each segment of the industry is dependent upon the other. The manufacturers produce products such as golf clubs, baseball bats, and shoes that individuals will use to participate in leisure or organized sporting activities. These sporting activities are classified as services offered by a variety of sport organizations as their main consumer commodity. Concurrently, many service providers offer products to their customers at or in conjunction with events in the form of concessions, souvenirs, or items from a pro shop.

Differentiating Products and Services

Although products and services are intermixed in sport marketing, there are market-relevant characteristics that need to be understood. Arnott (1998) commented that the products and the methods companies use for marketing them are widely applied across businesses, but a product is not identical to a service. "The difference is important, because products are marketed and sold differently than are services" (Arnott , 1998, p. 39).

Because sport services are such a large portion of the industry, it is important to understand the service environment. According to Hightower, Brady, and Baker (2002), the special nature of sports services shows that customers are influenced as much by the affective factors of the experience as its utility. As such, most sport venues pay significant attention to the environment—beyond simply fielding a competitive team—by providing music, pleasant surroundings, high quality food, and entertainment. Customer satisfaction in the service sector is based on the differences between service expectation and actual delivery. A questionnaire was developed in consort with The Ranch (sport arena) management based on four SERVQUAL dimensions encompassing the core criteria that customers utilize in evaluating service quality. It is reasonable, based on previous research, to speculate that consumers would consider all four dimensions important. Therefore, the critical measurement is the relationship between performance and expectations. At the end of the chapter is a survey used in customer satisfaction with services provided at a regional sports events center.

McDonald and Sutton's (1995) research in pro sports (specifically, the Orlando Magic) indicated that service quality is measure in four dimensions. This approach is supported by the work in Major League Baseball by Hightower, Brady, and Baker (2002, p. 698), who indicated, "[A] customer's service quality perceptions are influenced by their interaction with employees (i.e., functional quality), the perceived outcome of the service encounter (technical quality), and the firm's physical environment." McDonald and Sutton's dimensions:

Tangibles—physical facilities (e.g., colors, seat width, bathroom lines), equipment, appearance of personnel;

Reliability—performance of the service dependably and accurately;

Responsiveness—willingness to help customers and provide prompt service;

Empathy—attention and perceived "caring" about the customer.

Hightower et al. (2002) found that the service environment is critical to customers' intention to repeat as customers. They also found that "perceptions of stadium quality are directly and positively related to excitement and indirectly linked to repatronage intentions" (p. 699).

Products and services differ in that products are typically produced, distributed, and then purchased. At times, because of the retailing chain, producers lack direct contact with consumers. Products have a physical presence that customers can touch, feel, and see. Because production, distribution, and consumption often occur at the same time, services cannot be inventoried, and unused capacity is lost forever (Pride & Ferrell, 2008). Therefore, some important distinctions must be accounted for in marketing planning.

Take for example a professional basketball game. The tickets are pre-sold, and the event is produced and consumed simultaneously. Therefore, no distribution is necessary. Some organizations choose to distribute through additional avenues such as radio and television, but these are arranged prior to the production of the event. Other sport services are produced only on demand. A fitness center operates programs at scheduled times, but offers personal training on an on-demand basis. Sports medicine clinics provide another example of services that are made available on demand.

One of the most important aspects of sport marketing, in contrast to traditional business marketing, is that the sport service is often intangible (Mullin, Hardy, & Sutton, 2007; Pride & Ferrell, 2008). Why did this person come to the game? One may jump to the conclusion that it was to witness the promoted sports event. This is not necessarily true. Could that person have come just to be with friends? How about just to enjoy the stadium setting? Could it be that they wanted to get away from their children for an evening and that the sporting event was a convenient excuse? Finally, could some of the spectators come for halftime entertainment or the food at the concession stand? Clearly, these possible consumer motivation factors must be of concern to sport marketers.

As presented above, few sport organizations market a single product or service. The central or "core" product is not often hard to describe, yet various supplementary goods or services known as *product extensions* often enhance it. Many sport organizations have found that a substantial amount of money can be generated from items such as concessions and souvenirs. At the U.S. Open (golf), organizers sold $10 million in merchandise, starting with 100,000 hats, accompanied by golf shirts ranging from $50 to $150 (Christie, 2004). Does this mean that they are in the souvenir industry? No, it means that they have implemented product extensions to gain additional revenues or to enhance the main product or service that they produce.

This leads us to the question, "What business are you in?" Although this may seem like an unusual question, it has a significant impact on the marketing of products. Often, the initial approach to answering this question is to reexamine the mission statement referred to in Chapter 1. A fitness center may fit in the health and fitness industry, yet its customers may perceive socialization as a major benefit. School sports programs fit in the business of education, but their main competition may be the entertainment businesses. Kotler and Armstrong (2006) refer to this circumstance as *marketing myopia*. Their example of the railroad industry provides considerable insight into this phenomenon. The railroads did not fall into decline because there was a lack of need for their services; rather, railroad executives saw themselves in the railroad business, not in the transportation industry. Consequently, much of their business was taken by trucking, shipping, and airfreight companies.

An example of this concept in the sports service sector can be found in the stadium/arena management area. Many municipalities and universities traditionally hired outside companies to run the concession aspect of their operations. In the late 1980s, these companies began to see themselves in the arena management business, not just in food service. As a result, the 1990s produced a situation where corporations like SMG, ARAMARK, and Global Spectrum grew into major corporations by managing facilities as well as food services. Founded in 1977, SMG currently manages 69 arenas, 7 stadiums, 49 convention centers, 33 performing arts centers, and 10 other recreational facilities around the globe (http://www.smgworld.com/, 2008). ARAMARK began life in 1936 as a vending machine service company. It is now engaged in food service operations, venue management, and a variety of other service industries to more than 130 premier sports stadiums, arenas, and concert venues across the country. It has over 250,000 employees in 19 different countries with annual revenues of $16 billion. Global Spectrum began operations in 1994 as Globe Facility Services. In January 2000, a majority interest in Globe Facility Services was acquired by Comcast-Spectacor, creating one of the leading and best financially resourced private management companies in the industry. Global Spectrum's parent company, Comcast-Spectacor, is the Philadelphia-based sports and entertainment firm that owns the Philadelphia Flyers of the National Hockey League, the Philadelphia 76's of the National Basketball Association, the Wachovia Center, the Wachovia Spectrum, and Comcast Sports Net, the 24-hour regional sports programming TV network. Comcast-Spectacor also includes Ovations Food Services and Patron Solutions, a company offering a new and unique approach to in-house ticketing services (http://www.global-spectrum.com/, 2008).

Core Products and Product Extensions

How then does an organization determine the exact business in which to be engaged? The cornerstone of marketing is the provision of goods and services to meet consumer needs. Businesses often perceive themselves to be producers of goods and services. The business in which you engage is, therefore, defined in terms of consumers. This does not present a conflict unless the goods or services produced do not meet the needs of consumers. Marketing scholars and researchers continually argue over whether consumer needs can be created or if marketers must lead consumers to the realization of their needs. The historical example of John D. Rockefeller sending free kerosene lamps to China in order to create a need for his oil company's products is widely known and shows that in some cases consumer needs can be manipulated.

Sport organizations need to examine whether they have the approach of meeting consumer needs or are producing goods and services in hopes that someone will purchase them. Once an organization decides what business they are in, it is well on its way to marketing its business. Engaging in sport marketing requires a realization that success lies in identifying and meeting consumer needs, not just producing products or services with the hope of acceptance and consumption. Subsequent chapters of this workbook will assist in determining who those consumers may be and in identifying and creating products and services to meet their needs.

This occurs primarily through what has been traditionally referred to as the marketing mix. Marketing decisions can be based on the four basic elements—product, price, place, and promotion (4 Ps of Marketing). This framework was originally developed in the 1960s and has been renamed, repackaged, and otherwise used in the profession for many years but essentially remains in use throughout the industry. However, the approach is framed from the company or selling perspective. The 4 C approach—customer solution, customer cost, convenience, and communication—takes a more buyer-oriented perspective (Kotler & Armstrong, 2006).

Experience Marketing

According to Hill, Pine, Gilmore, Betts, Houmann, and Stubblefield (2001, p. 44), "Experiences are a distinct economic offering as distinct from services as services are from goods, but one that, until now, went largely unrecognized. When someone buys a good, he receives a tangible thing; when he buys a service, he purchases a set of intangible activities carried out on his behalf. But when he buys an experience, he pays for a memorable event that a company stages to engage him in an inherently personal way." Contemporary examples of the experience economy can be seen in Disney theme parks, Starbucks Coffee shops and, in sports, at Recreational Equipment Inc.'s (REI) trademark stores. Interior and exterior decorating is normally easy to change or design to suit an organization's needs. REI initiated a unique marketing experience approach in many of its western US stores. Each store (generally located near a shopping mall) creates the environment with a climbing site. On their way in, customers walk past the climbing wall (many replete with faux stone) with several climbing courses attached. This allows consumers to test REI equipment and creates the image of being in the "outdoors," even though it is a 10,000 sq. ft. store. In addition, REI stores provide a variety of settings for instruction and product testing, such as trying rain gear in a simulated rainstorm or ski parkas and sleeping bags in a "cold room"(Kotler, 2003; Pride & Ferrell, 2008). Much of sports is about the experience—getting the customer involved. Whether it is buying a pair of shoes at a Niketown Store, working with a personal trainer at a health club, or watching a game in a stadium, it is all about the experience. Success in experience marketing is about exceeding the customer's expectations and creating a "magical" encounter.

McCarthy's 4 Ps of Marketing

Traditional marketing, the 4 P's of marketing as coined by E. Jerome McCarthy (McCarthy & Perreault, 1990), specifically refers to the following:

Product: The nature of the product or service, including decisions as to a product line, product extensions, and meeting new consumer needs within the designated group of customers.

Price: A fair price that also reflects the image you want to portray about your product or service. Considerations include competitor's prices, available discounts, and market share.

Place: The actual distribution of your product or service. This could include means of transporting goods to wholesale and retail outlets or references to the geographic location of your stadium or health club.

Promotion: Getting your message about products and services to potential consumers. This can be attained through publicity, advertising, or other means of communication.

Each of these marketing mix elements receives additional attention throughout this book. Pitts and Stotlar (2007) provide a detailed overview of the topics included in this chapter in *Fundamentals of Sport Marketing*. As previously mentioned, none of these marketing elements work in isolation. Contemporary marketing leaders discuss the dynamics that exist in today's marketing environment and contend that all marketing elements and marketing communications must be fully integrated to be effective.

Integrated Marketing

Iacobucci and Calder (2003, p. xvi) note, "The challenge for the marketing organization in the twenty-first century is to combine traditional marketing, much of which is still very relevant in both sophisticated and emerging markets, with new approaches offered by electronic systems. It is a combined, converging, interactive, inter-connected, and networked system of customers, marketers, distributors, and technology that challenges today's marketing organization." Each of the elements can be further activated through specified marketing strategies and tactics. What follows in subsequent chapters is an overview of these dynamics.

Below is a survey used in research for a regional events center to measure customer satisfaction. The research results were used to modify the environment and the events to improve satisfaction.

Larimer County Fairgrounds and Events Complex
Customer Satisfaction Survey

The Larimer County Fairgrounds and Events Complex (aka The Ranch) is interested in obtaining feedback on the events and services offered to make your experience the best possible. Please take a few moments to complete this questionnaire. Your responses will be completely confidential. Thank you for your assistance.

Please rate the following amenities for quality and service as they apply to services *you encountered*.

Please Circle (1 = Strongly Agree, 2 = Agree, 3 = No Opinion, 4 = Disagree, 5 = Strongly Disagree). Also rate the importance of each of these areas to you (1 = Very Important, 2 = Somewhat Important, 3 = Not Important).

	SA	Agree	NO	Disagree	SD	VI	SI	NI
Reliability								
The Ranch staff provided services as promised.	1	2	3	4	5	1	2	3
The Ranch staff was dependable in handling my problems.	1	2	3	4	5	1	2	3
The Ranch staff performed their service right the first time.	1	2	3	4	5	1	2	3
The Ranch employees were well trained and knowledgeable.	1	2	3	4	5	1	2	3
Responsiveness								
The Ranch staff gave me prompt service.	1	2	3	4	5	1	2	3
The Ranch staff was always willing to help me.	1	2	3	4	5	1	2	3
There were enough Ranch staff members to respond to my requests.	1	2	3	4	5	1	2	3
The Ranch staff gave me individual attention.	1	2	3	4	5	1	2	3
Personalization								
Everyone at The Ranch was polite and courteous.	1	2	3	4	5	1	2	3
The Ranch employees were warm and friendly.	1	2	3	4	5	1	2	3
The Ranch employees took the time to know me personally.	1	2	3	4	5	1	2	3

Satisfaction Survey (cont.)	SA	Agree	NO	Disagree	SD	VI	SI	NI

Tangibles

	SA	Agree	NO	Disagree	SD	VI	SI	NI
The Ranch venue has comfortable seating areas.	1	2	3	4	5	1	2	3
The Ranch's physical facilities are visually appealing	1	2	3	4	5	1	2	3
Access to facilities was well marked and easy to navigate.	1	2	3	4	5	1	2	3
The Ranch's employees had a neat and professional appearance.	1	2	3	4	5	1	2	3
Materials associated with this event (such as brochures, tickets, or advertisements) were clear and correct.	1	2	3	4	5	1	2	3

Intangibles

	Excel	Good	Ave.	Below Ave.	Poor
The overall quality of the event itself was	1	2	3	4	5
The overall quality of the service at this event was	1	2	3	4	5
Overall, my satisfaction with this facility was	1	2	3	4	5
Overall, attention to my safety was	1	2	3	4	5

	Definitely	Maybe	Probably Not
Would you recommend this event to friends?	1	2	3
If there was another event that you could go to, would you?	1	2	3

Including today, how many times have you attended events at The Ranch? _____

The worksheets provide a guide for developing various sections of a marketing plan. The following sheets cover the areas of value proposition, product and service analysis, and determining the primary business sector in which an organization plans to conduct business. Complete these worksheets as a preliminary step in the creation of a marketing plan.

Value Proposition Worksheets

Specify the mission statement of the business for which the marketing plan is based.

_____

_____

_____

_____

_____

_____

_____

_____

_____

_____

_____

Explain the value proposition, including the products or services to be marketed.

_____
_____
_____
_____
_____
_____
_____
_____
_____
_____

Describe projected core products.

_____
_____
_____
_____
_____
_____
_____
_____
_____
_____

Project possible product extensions.

_____
_____
_____
_____
_____
_____
_____
_____
_____

Determine the primary business sector in which you will operate.

_____
_____
_____
_____
_____
_____

_____

_____

_____

Describe the experience "touch points" you anticipate with your product/service.

_____

_____

_____

_____

_____

_____

_____

_____

Describe how you will plan for full integration of your marketing activities.

_____

_____

_____

_____

_____

_____

_____

_____

Chapter Three

UNDERSTANDING THE MARKET ENVIRONMENT

Situation Analysis and Market Factors

Marketing authorities agree that marketers need to examine total market conditions and maintain both the marketing environment and consumers (Kotler & Armstrong, 2006). A situation analysis of the market provides facts and information necessary for planning and implementing the marketing mix. No sport organization exists in a static environment; there is a constant state of change that necessitates ongoing analysis. Moore (1998) reported that many leaders in sport marketing firms are noting the value of market research: "As sport has matured into a more sophisticated and expensive business, the demand for accurate market research has grown as well" (p. 12). Recognizing and adapting to this change can make a difference in whether or not an organization can grow and prosper or is destined to die like the estimated 90% of new business ventures in this country (Pride & Ferrell, 2008). In short, the best business marketing decisions are made when they are based on the best data.

According to Cohen (1998), the following elements must be examined in order to perform a valid situation analysis: economic climate, demographics, demand trends, technological trends, competitor analysis, and internal status of the company. McDonald and Keegan (2003) refer to the process as conducting a "market audit." These and other elements are discussed in greater detail in *Fundamentals of Sport Marketing* (Pitts & Stotlar, 2007).

ECONOMIC CLIMATE

Products and services perform differently in different economic environments. Some do well in inflationary periods, while others flourish in recessions. In 1998, serious economic turmoil occurred in Asian markets due to a significant financial downturn. Substantial repercussions were realized across many sport markets, events, and sponsorship arrangements. In response to the economic decline, a considerable amount of organizational activity occurred in "downsizing" sport enterprises across the United States. Companies were focused on profits and seemed to have limited emphasis on long-term benefits. Stevens, Loudon, Wrenn, and Warren (1997) indicated that this strategy, while reducing some operating costs, often resulted in significant losses in competitive marketing advantages. Their belief is that, over the next 20 years, corporations will need to focus more on marketing planning and strategy.

The sport industry is particularly vulnerable to changes in the economy because it is based on discretionary income. That is, no sport or sport-related product or service is a necessity (as are food, water, housing, or medical care). This makes it essential to keep a close watch on economic forecasts and to use the information to make wise marketing decisions.

Finally, an additional economic factor that is vitally important to running a successful business is the interest rate for borrowed monies. A large number of sport enterprises are capital intensive. They must borrow large sums of money to build facilities or purchase equipment. A change in one percentage point on a loan can make several thousand dollars difference in repayment schedules. The cost of financing is therefore critical in determining the ability to show a profit.

LEGAL ENVIRONMENT

Federal tax laws have also played a major role in sport marketing in the US. The 1988 Tax Reform Act seriously decreased the amount companies could deduct for the purchase of "sky boxes" and scholarship programs that included tickets. An NCAA ruling in 1998 profoundly affected sporting goods manufacturers. The NCAA, reacting to safety concerns, passed legislation restricting the barrel size of aluminum bats to 2 3/4 inches. As a result, Rawlings Sporting Goods was forced "to dump thousands of bats it [had] already produced, costing the company $400,000" (Kaplan, 1998, p. 14).

Laster (2004) discussed another organizationally imposed set of standards that greatly affected the industry:

> What started in 2000 with the Amateur Softball Association of America's (ASA) adoption of a bat performance standard in slow-pitch softball has snowballed into one of the biggest issues facing dealers and manufacturers today. The standard, based on batted ball speed (BBS) takes into account the swing speed of the bat and the pitch speed of the ball. ASA's standard seeks to place a maximum limit on how fast a ball can come off a bat. In 2000, ASA set a maximum BBS limit of 125 feet per second, using the then-industry standard ASTM F1890 standard test method, which was developed by the American Society of Testing and Materials. Any bat found to be in non-compliance with the BBS limit was deemed unacceptable, would not be awarded the ASA's official certification decal and could not be used in any ASA games or events. (Laster, 2004, p. 3)

When ASA changed the rules again in 2002, dealers and manufacturers were a bit peeved. The new standard, which took effect in January 2004, included a maximum BBS limit of 98 mph when tested with the new ASTM F2219 test method (F1890 is no longer the standard). All manufacturers whose bats exceeded ASA's limits were recalled, retrofitted, and shipped back to dealers. Manufacturers were receiving bats starting in the fall of 2002 all the way up to the summer of 2003. It was obviously time-consuming and costly to ship them to be retrofitted and then return them, all at company expense. And some of the models went back five or six years.

The legal environment also includes the political environs that affect economics. In 1989, the United States and Canada entered into a free trade agreement, which reduced and eliminated many previously imposed tariffs. If an organization was contemplating creating a product to compete with a Canadian firm, the price comparison could have been substantially affected by this act. The issue arose once again in 2005 when the Congress passed the Central American Free Trade Agreement, extending the same regulations across Central America. In 2002, President George W. Bush sought to protect the US steel industry by imposing tariffs on imported raw steel and that decision had a significant impact on one US sports manufacturer: Goalsetters. The company manufactures portable basketball standards, and the new tariffs substantially raised the cost of their materials. They were forced to consider raising prices to maintain their profit margins. However, another option was to stop making their products in the US and move manufacturing offshore. This had the opposite effect Bush intended on the economy. Because only the raw materials were taxed and not fully assembled products, the US lost jobs when the assembly work went overseas. In another act important to sport professionals, the U.S. Congress passed the Get Outdoors Act in 2004. The act provided annual allocations of $450 million for improving parks and recreation facilities, stimulating spending in that segment of the industry. It is clear that attention must be paid to political circumstances, both in the US and globally.

Another rather odd political impact on sport marketing occurred in 2006 when the National Park Service issued new guidelines on advertising in national parks. All advertising had previously been prohibited, but now "temporary" advertising would be allowed as approved. This would impact anyone selling signage for triathlon or cross-country ski events that utilized park service land.

The formation and liberalization that took place within the European Community in 1992 also brought many challenges and opportunities in sport. This event dramatically affected the sport industry. Of specific concern to professional sport organization was the free movement of labor. Article 48 of the Treaty of Rome states that members of States have the right to work and live in member States. In European sports, this meant a free and open market for all athletes, and bidding wars were prevalent. Another area of concern surfaced in sports equipment. Manufacturers in England were required to follow one set of product safety codes, while France had another. The EC unification, therefore, brought serious issues to bear on sporting goods companies from both an economic and legal perspective.

Sport organizations in the business of providing services are generally labor intensive, with the majority of their expenses arising from payroll costs and the associated benefit plans. Changing legislation in this sector could dictate fluctuations in the minimum wage, social security payments, worker's compensation, and benefit costs.

Another legal concern arises when corporate marketers decide to associate their company with sport events without paying associated sponsorship fees. This tactic has become known as "ambush marketing." Ambush marketing is "a promotional strategy whereby a non-sponsor attempts to capitalize on the popularity/prestige of a property by giving the false impression that it is a sponsor. [This tactic is] often employed by the competitors of a property's official sponsors" (Ukman, 1995, p. 42). Several examples of ambush marketing have occurred within the sport industry.

During the 1984 Olympic Games, Nike, not an official sponsor, had murals painted on the sides of assorted downtown Los Angeles buildings (Myerson, 1996). The same strategy was averted in Atlanta when the City Council passed a ban on large-scale outdoor advertising. Reebok officials unsuccessfully argued that their proposed 60-by-80 foot mural of Shaquille O'Neal was public art (Bayor, 1996).

American Express and VISA have had continuous legal battles over legitimate Olympic sponsorship rights and alleged ambush tactics since 1988. VISA aired advertising that claimed that the Olympics would not take American Express cards. While accurate regarding the official ticket outlets, various tour companies and other travel-related services would accept American Express cards in payment for travel to the Olympic Games. The International Olympic Committee has become very aggressive in fighting ambush marketing and the incidences of the tactic during subsequent Olympic Games have been minuscule.

In one situation, Pebble Beach golf course sued another golf course, Tour 18, which opened a course that replicated famous holes from PGA courses (e.g., Pebble Beach). No permission was received from these courses, and their protected logos were used liberally around the course and on the clubhouse menu. While it would be difficult to show the likelihood of confusion, a stipulation required under trademark law, it was argued that use of logos implied permission. Also, the PGA claimed that the "design elements" of each hole are protectable under copyright law. The court ruled that use of logos amounted to misappropriation of a property right. Specific design elements were found not to be protectable (Pebble Beach v. Tour 18, 942 F. Supp 1513).

DEMOGRAPHICS

The characteristics of a population are referred to as demographics or a consumer's state of being. This can include such factors as age, gender, marital status, lifestyle, occupation, and earned income. The exact proportion of any one segment in the nation or in a specific community changes periodically. Demographic changes in the US population are drastically changing sport marketing. All of the major sports leagues are peppered with international players. Subsequently, sport marketers are targeting international fans for their sport. The NBA conducted 36 international events in 214 countries across 6 continents and is broadcast in 43 languages. The international scope of the NBA can be seen with more than 80 international players from 35 different countries and territories, and the trend is growing at 30% per year. To further illustrate the power of NBA basketball, 8 out of 10 international teens could recognize the NBA logo (Mullin et. al., 2006).

"Population trends have forced teams to take a hard look at marketing efforts. However, teams and leagues have found that there's no one correct approach. In fact, while marketers often discuss how to reach Hispanic or Asian consumers, those labels themselves oversimplify the challenge" (Brenner, 2004, pp. 15–16).

Evidence of this is represented by the NBA, whose Miami office has employees representing several Latin American countries.

Sport marketers must be cognizant of these changes, as well as the percentages of certain groups that make up a target market. Succeeding chapters of this workbook and *Fundamentals of Sport Marketing* (Pitts & Stotlar, 2007) address target markets in greater detail, but a brief discussion is needed at this point. The target market is that specific group of customers that the marketer feels will be most likely to purchase the product or service being offered.

The shared characteristics of a target market can be compared in the process of situational analysis. In a general sense, knowing the proportion of any given segment that may be available to the marketer is certainly important. For example, if a sport product is marketed to customers who are 12–15 years old, a marketer would want to know how many individuals that particular section of the population included. On the other hand, if services are aimed at retired persons, the data on that group would also be important.

This information is rather easy to find. Several companies engage in market research for the entire country and publish their data in magazines and special reports. These are usually available in public libraries. One such publication is S&MM (formerly Sales & Marketing Management). Its issue on consumer buying power is exceptionally useful. The guide lists different geographical areas, identifies the population by age, income, and purchasing activity, and calculates their effective buying power. If you wanted to know the percentage of people in the 25–34 year old age group in Denver, you could see that it was 22.9%. This could be compared to any other city in the country or even examined on a county basis within the city (S&MM, 2004). All of these data can be collected and/or reviewed by the sport organization and will play a part in the development of the marketing plan.

As discussed earlier, it is important to recognize sport-related needs that these groups have in order to develop new products or highlight aspects of existing products that would appeal to recognizable groups.

DEMAND TRENDS

The American economy is governed by supply and demand—in the vernacular, "what's hot, what's not." Any sport venture that explores new products or markets new services takes sizable risks. As noted earlier, the estimated rate at which new businesses fail is about 90% (Pride & Ferrell, 2008). Yet, many successful sports products have been established on the mere hope that there will be a demand.

For example, who could have predicted the phenomenal success of Wham-o Corporation's Frisbee? Was there a clear demand trend for this product? Probably not. Who would have thought that a track coach working in his basement designing a shoe with a waffle style sole (Nike) would succeed in the athletic footwear business? However, there may have been a clear demand trend for a lightweight training shoe with features similar to those used for racing. And what about the jogging and general fitness trends? These people would need something to put on their feet.

Predictions of demand are not without peril. An industry marketing firm, Sports Marketing and Retail Technology, incorrectly predicted significant increases in the ski industry for an upcoming year. What happened to thwart their prediction? It didn't snow.

The ski industry also changed in terms of the type of product in demand in the late 1980s. Something called a snowboard was introduced to the market. In fact, some ski areas actually contemplated banning snowboards from their ski areas. The rest, as they say, is history. Additional changes surfaced in the 1990s. Jones (1989) indicated that ski customers were no longer intent on purchasing their own equipment. Because most skiers are tourists or are only occasional skiers, the economy of purchasing an $800 pair of skis came into question. Renting a pair of high performance skis would run only about $50 per day, and the customer could come back next year and have a brand new set with the latest style and color. In addition, they didn't have to carry their skis to and from the airport.

PRODUCT LIFE CYCLE

Most products and services can be plotted on a life cycle chart similar to the one shown here. This typically starts with the introduction to the consumer, then shows moderate growth in both sales and profits, increasing through the growth stage, leveling during maturity, and falling during the decline phase. Industries also follow life cycles.

In the mid-1980s, the fitness industry encountered two significant problems—falling demand for its services and an overabundance of clubs. As a result, many fitness centers and health clubs were forced out of business. If the managers could have predicted this turn of events, they may have offered new services or products to their clients or even targeted previously untapped customers. The Sporting Goods Manufacturers Association provides an excellent source for this type of data (www.sgma.com). For instance, their data showed that over the period from 2000–2006, participation in high-impact aerobics fell 25.9%. In contrast, lifting

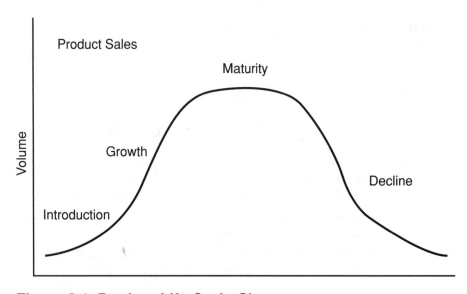

Figure 3.1. Product Life Cycle Chart

free weights rose 76% and became the number one ranked fitness activity. Thus, fitness centers could analyze the trends, make adjustments in the programs and services offered, and more precisely plan future equipment purchases.

Similarly, many companies introduce new products as old ones are dying out. The words "new and improved" are familiar to today's consumer. It may be of interest to know that the use of the word "new" is actually regulated by the US government. The Federal Trade Commission (FTC) specifies that for a product to be tagged "new" it must either be totally redesigned or different in a functionally significant manner. In the sport industry, that would make introducing a "new" basketball extremely difficult. In addition, the FTC restricts the use of the term "new" to a period of six months. The Boston Consulting Group pioneered a marketing management matrix based on product life cycles. They classified products into four categories based on their marketing characteristics. *Stars* are products that have high market share and a high potential for growth and are therefore deserving of investment. *Cash Cows* are those products with a high market share, in a maturity stage, thus generating considerable profits without need of significant investment. *Questions Marks* are those products that currently have a low market share but have the potential to increase their share and profits if investments are provided. These products can move in one of two directions. If successful, they become stars; if not, they become *Dogs*. *Dogs* are products characterized by low growth and low market share. They do not merit additional infusions of either funds or effort (Kotler & Armstrong, 2006).

The job of the marketer is to determine at what point his or her product or service resides in a particular cycle or category. Although accurate prediction of any or all phases is difficult, considerable effort should be put forth to do so. *Dogs* are the most troubling products because of their drain on resources (both capital and human), and someone is always touting a big turnaround. Be wary; mistakes can be likened to jumping on a sinking ship.

One interesting example of market timing involved Reebok's concentration on the escalating aerobic shoe market in the 1980s. Thoroughly missed by Nike, Reebok's revenues went from $4 million in 1984 to $900 million in 1988 (Rudolph, 1989). Another example of industry rise and decline can be seen in the sales of licensed sports merchandise. During the 1980s and early 1990s, the market for licensed merchandise rose over 300%, only to fall precipitously in the late 1990s when a decline in demand coincided with over–supply. The under-15 market stopped buying team logo jackets in favor of the "grunge" or "surfer" look.

The late 1990s also displayed changes in fashion trends reflected in the sales of athletic footwear. After years of setting record sales levels, the two leading athletic shoemakers saw their share of the shoe market fall substantially. What had once been "in fashion" was suddenly "out." Similarly, Doc Martens, Sketchers, and Tevas replaced athletic shoes as the product of choice for the younger market.

It is critical for marketing plans to accurately reflect market research on the latest trends and enable managers to respond quickly to changes in the sport industry. Assessing a demand trend is difficult, but help can be obtained in several forms. Many trade associations and their publications analyze and research trends in the industry. Organizations such as the International Health, Racquet & Sportsclub Association, the Association for Fitness in Business, the National Sporting Goods Manufacturers Association, and Amusement Business magazine all provide information about specific industries that can help you predict coming demand and product trends. For example, the Sporting Goods Manufacturer's Association reported that athletic footwear and sports apparel grew of an average 2.7% per year for 2003–2007 (www.smga.com, 2007). The total global sporting goods market was estimated to be $256 billion.

TECHNOLOGICAL TRENDS

The impact of science and technology on sports products and services varies greatly. Rapid technological change has marked the last decade and, in fact, the last century. What will the future hold? Although there are no pat answers, the sport marketer should be aware of upcoming industry trends. In the sporting goods industry, much of this is accomplished through the research and development departments of the major corporations.

These research activities contributed to the British rowing team in the 2004 Athens Olympic Games. The British Olympic rowing team called on a small Pennsylvania-based company, Noble Fiber Technologies, to create uniforms that would diffuse the intense Greek heat. Noble developed a technology to adhere pure silver to a basic textile, which allows the fabric to take on the chemical properties of silver. The fiber is not only for Olympic athletes; Noble has also secured licensee agreements with sportswear manufacturers Umbro and Adidas (Lake, 2004). Similarly, swim suit manufacturer Speedo created the LZR Racing suit for the 2008 Olympics. It reportedly has 10% less drag than Speedo's FASTSKIN FSII and 5% less passive drag than Speedo's FASTSKIN PRO, which swimmers have worn in breaking 21 world records since its introduction in March 2007.

Trade shows offer the average person a chance to see the newest in product development. Recent advances in tennis rackets, shoes, golf clubs, and other sport products create an environment in which effective marketing practices are not enough; companies must deliver on performance as well.

One of the complaints about aluminum baseball bats was that the excessive vibrations hurt players' hands. Enter vibration technology. The technology first appeared in fighter planes to reduce vibrations. Manufacturers were investigating methods to reduce the vibrations in their bats when they discovered this space-age technology. Incorporating the technology in bats will raise the price of the bats to between $279–299 but may offer better results. The technology also complied with new safety requirements proposed by the NCAA and other baseball organizations, while increasing the "sweet spot" on the barrel (http://www.eastonsoftball batsbaseballbats.com).

Is the sophistication of a product increasing, or is there a demand for a less complicated product? Many fitness centers in the early 1990s rushed out to buy the newest computerized gadgets and machines, yet some of their clients preferred standard Olympic lifting equipment. By 2004, lifting "free" weights had become the top ranked fitness activity, outpacing stationary activities. Lauer (2006) notes that equipment trends heavily favor user-friendly equipment. Without closely supervising and monitoring technological trends and customers, expensive mistakes can be made.

But what of the service industry? How does technology affect those services? There may well be new amenities needed at a sport facility. At the 1998 Super Bowl in San Diego, Vyvx Services equipped 400 seats with 10 "video monitors (Smart Seats) that could be used by patrons to access game statistics and review the game and replays from as many as nine different camera angles (Williams, 1998). According to Morrell (2004, p. 42), "It didn't fail because of problems with the product—the technology moved on very quickly." This technology expanded with the proliferation of wireless technology. In 2004, the San Francisco Giants created a wireless (Wi-Fi) network at SBC Park. The so-called "digital dugout" allows fans to access real-time player statistics and replays from a variety of camera angles (Haner, 2004). This and other applications of technology are commonplace today and have proven to be critical to facility management and marketing.

Computer assisted distribution through automated ticket outlets may well place an organization in an advantageous market position. Several companies have developed around providing these technological services. Additional information will be provided on this topic in Chapter 7 in the discussion on product distribution. In general, these technological advances enable the sport enterprises to operate more efficiently and give better service to their customers. Technology, therefore, can affect your sport enterprise and create marketing opportunities.

Competitor Analysis

It is said that imitation is the sincerest form of flattery; however, in business, it is not considered quite as noble. For example, the organizer of the New York marathon scheduled a trip to Los Angeles to "steal ideas" from the directors of the L.A. Marathon on sport marketing (Cole, 1988, p. 43). The list of look-a-likes and sound-a-likes in any industry is long. Although most sport organizations attempt to present unique images, a certain amount of copying exists. The ski industry is noted for quick changes in style and color. If competitors see that one company's ideas are selling well, their products are soon arrayed in similar colors and can be found in similar designs.

In many organizations, studying the competition is critical to business success. My college fraternity brother and teammate was Mike Shanahan, head coach of the Denver Broncos. In his book, *Think Like a Champion*, Mike says, "It baffles me that so many people fail to counter what their competitors are doing. It's right in front of them and they're somehow blind to it" (Shanahan, 1999, p. 106).

However, marketing experts Kotler and Armstrong (2006, p. 544) contend that "a company can become so competitor-centered that it loses its even more important focus on maintaining profitable customer relationships." Keeping an eye on the competition is ethical and legal. A variety of ways have been suggested to assist you in this process:

1. Buy your competitors' products. This may mean some expense, but valuable

ideas can be achieved. This also can mean attending their contests, visiting their fitness center, or hiring their services.

2. Frequent your competitors' territories. Often, new ideas and trade secrets are overheard in casual conversations.

3. Read the right publications as mentioned earlier from industry organizations such as the International Health, Racquet & Sportsclub Association, the Association for Fitness in Business, the Sporting Goods Manufacturers Association, and Amusement Business magazine.

4. Be careful not to get so caught up in this process that your own organization suffers due to lack of attention. (Eby, 1987)

Some sport management professionals conduct only limited research to identify who qualifies as a competitor. College and university sports teams often are quick to identify an archrival as their competitor. This, however, is not usually the case. Do you compete for the same customers? Would people go to their game if they were not coming to yours? It might be possible for the main competition to be movie theaters, shopping malls, or other community events. On the other hand, a network television station may choose between televising your game and the other game, and in this case, that game would be your direct competitor.

Clearly determining competitors is a difficult task. It starts with the planning and analysis discussed in the first two chapters of this workbook. Once identified, they should be studied. See what they are doing; try to assess their strategy in the market place. Each competitor has a different position in the market; each has its particular strengths and weaknesses. All of these are important considerations in marketing efforts.

Several publications can assist the retail sporting goods business. Most libraries contain business publications that provide information on the annual income, gross assets, and number of employees for leading manufacturers. Online publications and websites are a great source of information as well. Much of the information used in examining corporate profits and losses can be gleaned from annual reports filed by the company. The SEC (Securities and Exchange Commission) requires all publicly held companies in the US with over 500 shareholders and $10 million in assets to file annual reports. Information in these reports can be accessed through the SEC's website (http://www.sec.gov) and through the Public Register's Annual Report Service (http://www.prars.com). For example, adidas reported their sales volume increase of 14% in 2006 compared to 2005. For not-for-profit organizations [501(c) (3)] such as the USOC, the Internal Revenue Service requires them to file a 990 Form detailing their income and expenses. Many of the college football bowl organizations are also 501(c) (3)s. Through the IRS-990, you could find that the 2007 Outback Bowl had $9.9 million in revenues and expenses of $9.6 million, with their CEO collecting $498,000 in salary. Many of these reports can be located at www.guidestar.com.

Additional data on corporate finances and profits can be derived from a publication called the Market Share Reporter. This resource documents the percentage of a given market controlled by different companies. These types of information do not provide all of the answers to your analysis questions, but with the other actions mentioned above, they form a reliable base from which to begin. Again, Broncos coach Mike Shanahan commented, "Having a clear understanding of your competitor's strengths and weaknesses, their strategies and tactics, will provide you with a renewed feeling of confidence" (1999, p. 109).

SWOT Analysis

The process referred to as a SWOT analysis (Strengths, Weaknesses, Opportunities, and Threats) is similar to most game/strategy planning for sport teams. The initial step in the process is an extensive examination of your organization's strengths and weaknesses, followed by an identical evaluation of the competition's strengths and weaknesses. The highlights of a SWOT analysis on the Reebok post-adidas merger is provided in Table 3.1.

Table 3.1. Reebok SWOT Analysis with adidas merger

Internal Strengths
- Extremely strong financial position with adidas merger
- High level of liquidity
- Minimal long-term debt
- Access to financial and management resources through adidas merger
- Higher diversity than competitors
- Clear market leader in several product categories
- Established brand image of quality, technology, and prestige
- Favorable brand recognition
- Top management is market-oriented
- Favorable market demand trends

Internal Weaknesses
- High dependence on CEO
- Organizational change with adidas
- Recent turn-over in top management positions
- Weakness 2005 earning

Opportunities
- Market diversification and expansion into international markets based on adidas distribution and sales network
- Diversification and entry into multinational markets can prolong short product life cycles.
- Potential growth in the apparel market based on NFL, NBA, and NHL agreements

Threats
- NAFTA/CAFTA—may reduce price competitiveness of Reebok products manufactured in Asia directly affecting net income
- Strength of competitors
- Short product life cycles across the industry
- Possible weakening markets and brand equity
- Price escalation effecting consumer demand
- Potential for a weaker economy

Any attempt to measure systems components should be based on a set of established criteria. With SWOT, you must identify the criteria that will be used to evaluate your organization's strengths in the market. Suggested items could consist of product benefits, price, quality, availability, image, durability, distribution, personnel skills, manufacturing (or production) capacity, etc. To complete the next stage of a SWOT analysis, a rating system should be developed. In many sport organizations, this is more subjective than objective. Granted, an objective measure resulting from extensive market research is better, but some organizations use their own people to provide input based on their knowledge of the product or service. Research has discovered that customers utilize several criteria in making purchasing decisions in running shoes. Ninety-seven percent first consider fit and comfort, 83% consider injury prevention attributes, with a similar percentage examining the technological features of the shoes. Brand and price were ranked as the fourth and fifth most often considered factors, respectively (Rohn, 1997). Common rating systems could use either a continuum or a point scale to compare brands on these criteria. If one were to evaluate basketball shoes, an example could look like the one on the next page.

Feature: Comfort (hypothetical)

	Poor	Below Ave.	Average	Above Ave.	Excellent
Nike				X	
Reebok		X			
adidas					X
And1			X		
Fila	X				

Rating System Method (rating 1–5 with 5 being most favorable)

Feature: Technology (hypothetical)

Nike	5
Reebok	5
adidas	4
And1	4
Fila	1

Figure 3.2. Continuum Method

A very similar process could follow for each of the following components: competitors' strengths, organization's weaknesses, competitors' distribution weaknesses. Similar techniques can be used in developing "positioning" strategies for your products and services as discussed in Chapter 6.

The opportunities aspect of the SWOT approach is probably less understood than the other components. Opportunities stem from the ability of management to use its vision of the industry to determine how each strength can be used to the organization's advantage given current and predicted situational factors. Because prediction and vision are involved, this task is very subjective. It should also be nonjudgmental. This means that all possible opportunities that may exist should be explored. For example, the manufacturing capacity of one shoe company over another may be a strength, allowing it to produce more shoes faster; however, that may not be a strategy that is eventually selected. Opportunities for competitors must also be delineated. This can be accomplished by answering the question, "What would you see as opportunities for the organization if you were in their position?"

Threats are those problems that may adversely affect your organization (or the entire industry). Competitors can introduce new products, redesign existing products, or alter their pricing structures. Although it has been a common belief that "beating the competition" is a worthy business goal, a more contemporary view in marketing management is to make the competition meaningless. Stevens, Loudon, Wrenn, and Warren (1997, p. 117) indicated that the intent should not be to beat the competition but to "make competitors irrelevant to [your] customers."

The concept of making competitors irrelevant was developed into a strategy called the Blue Ocean strategy by Chan Kim and Renée Mauborgne (2004). Rather than competing against competitors in a red ocean, bloodied by competition, Kim and Mauborgne suggest that you can develop uncontested market space in a previously unknown or identified industry. One of the first examples in the sport industry (before the concept was labeled Blue Ocean) was Nike's creation of the Cross-

Trainer. After Nike missed the aerobics shoe explosion of the mid-80s, they created the Cross Trainer (replete with Nike funded research on multi-sport conditioning regimes to back it up). There were no other competitors, and Nike had uncontested market space. By the time other manufacturers developed competing products, Nike had secured the market and used revenues to promote their leadership in the newly created category.

A more recent example of Blue Ocean strategy is Cirque du Soleil. Founders Guy Laiberté and Daniel Gauthier, in 1984, banded together street performers and rein-vented the circus. Traditional circuses had issues with rising costs for performers and animal care and the protests over treatment of circus animals, coupled with uncom-fortable seating in dated venues with the "same old show." The Cirque du Soleil concept used modern-day gymnasts and dancers (in plentiful supply) to provide an exciting story-based show in the comforts of a theatre setting with dramatic light-ing and music. More fun than theatre, more exciting than the circus, and more comfortable than either, Cirque du Soleil became a cultural phenomenon. Presently, Cirque du Soleil employs 3,500 people from 40 countries and has a permanent stage in Las Vegas entertaining 9,000 people per night in addition to its fifteen tour-ing shows on every continent. In 2007, estimated annual revenue exceeded $600 million.

Internal Status of the Company

Every company has a unique chemistry that differentiates it from others. The em-ployees have special skills; the management, a certain vision; and the CEO, a per-sonal style. These unique assets can be classified as either strengths or weaknesses.

A true measurement of the skills of your staff is imperative. What kinds of attrib-utes do your workers have? Is your sales force better than others in the industry? Maybe your company has the advantages of longevity and a substantial percentage of your employees really knowing the organization. Normally in these situations, networking with established customers and business partners is a distinct advan-tage. Some segments of your staff may not be performing on a par with the com-petition. In such cases, a training program may be well worth the expense. In retail sporting goods manufacturing, you may have a technological advantage over your competitors. You could possibly have greater financial resources available for ex-pansion than your competition. Yet, weaknesses may be apparent in your channels of distribution. Your production capacity may be limited. The assessment of each of these components is essential. This is not to say that you should tear the organ-ization apart and begin laying blame, but rather, a fair and accurate measurement must take place prior to serious market planning. The implementation of market-ing strategy will help you turn the strengths into opportunities and also prevent weaknesses from becoming opportunities for your competition.

Any analysis is based on the current state of affairs. Certain assumptions are made based on economic indicators, existing technology, and the prevailing employee and management situation. Each of these assumptions should be noted so that a change in the status in any element would invoke a reexamination of the entire sce-nario. A sample situation analysis for a proposed golf driving range is provided at the end of this chapter for your review. No two organizations will conduct their analyses in the same manner. A custom fit, based on the essential information provided in this chapter, is therefore needed for each marketing project.

BEST PRACTICE

SITUATIONAL ANALYSIS

Proposed Denver West Gold Driving Range
Contributed by Dr. Kathy Malpass

SITUATIONAL ENVIRONS

America is awakening to the many enjoyable benefits of the game of golf. The pleasant three-mile walk with the relaxed company of friends makes for a great recreational activity. There is a new way of thinking about fitness and exercise in the eighties. Older adults and baby boomers are switching from activities like tennis and jogging, which are stressful to the joints, to alternatives such as walking and aquacise. The number of people playing golf has increased 10% to 25.7 million during the last five years. The numbers of beginning and junior golfers increased 30% during the last 10 years alone. It is anticipated that golfers will soon number 30 million. Women represent 42% of the new golfing population.

The American Society of Golf Course Architects has compiled data that one new golf course per day is needed by the year 2010 to satisfy the sport's growing needs. "Should financial institutions awaken to the fact that golf courses have proven to be good investments, especially public facilities, then some 400 courses per year would be put down," says Pete Dye, president of the architect's organization. "The development of quality public courses is essential to meet demands."

There is a growing need for all types of golf facilities, but especially for public golf courses and driving ranges. Today's golfer has a busy lifestyle, juggling job, family, and recreational activities. Golf facilities are adapting to these needs through various efforts to speed up play on the course and are gradually doing away with the antiquated "men's club" rules. A large percentage of women are in the workforce, creating a heavier demand for weekend play without restriction. Many working couples enjoy a round of golf together after work or on the weekend. Baby boomers have more money to spend on club dues and greens fees, as well as the need to entertain business clients. Increasing demands on leisure time and the desire to master this exciting and difficult game support the need for quality golf practice facilities.

Golf has traditionally been a game for the white upper class, just as skiing and polo have been. Better public facilities, many funded by municipalities, have helped bring the game to all races and economic levels. Golf appeals to a wide variety of age groups. The majority of golfers start the game in their late 20s and 30s and continue well into the "golden years." This is what makes golf so unique, "the game of a lifetime."

The Denver area has shown a strong need for additional golf facilities because a significant portion of the population is found in the 25–40 year old range. The median age for the geographic area of this study was found to be 33.4. Many of these baby boomers are taking up the game with a passion. Ranges at golf facilities in the geographic area are overcrowded with patrons waiting for a spot to hit range balls. Some of these facilities have had to require golfers to hit from mats because they cannot keep grass growing on the tees.

Getting good grass to grow has always been difficult in arid climates such as Denver. Horticulture specialists have developed several hardy varieties that do well with almost half the water that the popular Kentucky bluegrass requires. New housing developments are beginning to seed lawns with these new grasses, especially in the arid areas of Texas and Colorado. The high cost of water in the Denver area, in addition to the high amount of traffic by the golfers, would certainly encourage the possibility of seeding new driving ranges with one of these hardy grasses.

Perhaps one of the biggest roadblocks to building new golf facilities in the Denver area is political in nature. Many communities in Jefferson and Boulder counties have enacted legislation that prohibits new development. Unfortunately, golf courses are included in the same category as shopping centers and housing developments. The public needs to be educated that golf facilities are "open space" just like parks.

THE NEURAL ENVIRONS

The greatest hurdle in opening any new business is obtaining the necessary financial backing. Denver is suffering from an economic slowdown due to the oil industry and the unstable savings and loan institutions. The Small Business Administration and venture capital investors may provide other means for funding.

Both state and local agencies are working hard to bring new business into the Denver area. The local Golden Chamber of Commerce and the Jefferson County Planning and Zoning Office have traditionally been very helpful in assisting with these types of projects.

It is important in opening any new business that a positive image is presented to the media. All benefits of a quality golf practice facility should be stressed at every opportunity. Members of the media should be invited to visit the new facility with a complementary bucket of range balls and tips from the golf professional. Perhaps a "media day" could be organized with PGA and LPGA Tour stars available for tips and autographs.

Bad press and poor public rapport usually stem from misinformation and a lack of understanding. Special interest groups, such as the Jeffco Open Space Administration, should be invited to visit the facility so any concerns can be directly addressed.

COMPETITOR ENVIRONS

The main competitors to the Denver West Golf Range are 18-hole public golf courses with driving range facilities. The closest is Applewood Golf Course, located approximately two miles away, off of Route 58. The drive-by traffic is different from potential customers of Denver West Golf Range.

APPLEWOOD GOLF CLUB

14001 W. 32nd Avenue
Golden, Colorado 80401

Applewood Golf Course has recently been acquired by American Golf Corporation, a company that manages several golf facilities nationwide. The driving range was doubled in size, yet golfers still usually wait for a spot to hit range balls. Extensive other improvements have been made to both the golf course and the clubhouse since American Golf bought the facility.

Nearest competitor. Approximately 2 miles. No lights.

Driving Range:

   29 Astroturf mats on concrete
   2 tiered grass areas with a large fence dividing into 2 sides
   Small yardage signs at which to aim.
   Small putting green (poor condition)
   Pitching green with small sand trap
   (Golfers may use their own balls for this area.)

Prices:

   Medium bucket: $6.00
   Large bucket: $8.00
   Range ticket:
   10 baskets for $45.00 (AGC members)$60.00 (non-members)

FOOTHILLS GOLF COURSE

3901 S. Carr Street
Denver, Colorado 80226

Foothills Golf Course is an 18-hole public golf course with a Par-3 and a limited driving range facility. It is approximately 14 miles from the Denver West Golf Range, off of the 285 corridor. Foothills Golf course is owned and operated by the Foothills Recreation District. This district includes parts of Lakewood and Littleton. The driving range consists entirely of mats from which golfers hit. No grass tees are available. Golfers usually must wait for one of the 15 hitting tees to become available for practice.

Nearest competitor to the south. Approximately 14 miles. No lights, rubber mats only. Nine holes of Par-3.

Driving Range:

   15 rubber mats on concrete
   No grassed driving area
   Yardage signs at 100, 150, 200 yards
   Large putting green

Small pitching area with large practice sand trap
(Golfers may use their own balls for this area.)

Prices:

Warmup bag: $4.00
Regular bag: $6.00
Driving Range Pass: Buy 20 bags, get 5 free

Par 3:

Resident of Foothills Recreation District: $8.00
Non-resident: $10.00
Jr/Sr Weekday: $4.00

COMPANY ENVIRONS

Denver West Golf Range provides a quality practice facility in a very convenient location. There are 75 grass tees and 15 mat tees, a putting green, two sand traps, and a pitching area. The facility also includes an 18-hole miniature golf course and snack shop.

A variety of personalized services are provided at the Denver West Golf Range. Custom club-fitting and club repair are available year round. Video analysis of your swing, coaching for tournament play, and both group and private lessons are provided by PGA and LPGA professionals. Customers know they will consistently receive quality service at the Denver West Golf Range.

PLANNED DENVER WEST GOLF RANGE

1746 Old Golden Road
Golden, Colorado 80401

Driving Range

75 grass tees
15 mat tees
Yardage flags at 50, 75, 100, 125, 150, 175, 200, 225, 250 yards
Pitching area with flags at 25, 50, 75, 100 yards
Two sand traps with green landing area
Two putting greens in excellent condition

Prices:

small: $4.00
medium: $6.00
large: $8.00

Range Plan:

1. GREEN RANGE CARD: $60.00

11 large buckets for the price of 10
can repurchase (no limit)

2. GOLD RANGE CARD: $56.00

> 15 medium buckets for the price of 12
> For senior citizens who present GOLD CARD
> May be used 7:00 am–3:30 pm

3. SILVER RANGE CARD: $120.00

> 30 large buckets
> For Corporate memberships only
> Corporate Membership: $25.00
> Must have at least 5 members from the same company

Miniature Golf:

18 holes of miniature golf

Lighted until 11 p.m. (May 31–Sept 30)

Prices:

Children under 12: $2.00

Adults: $4.00

Other Competitors

Driving Range Only:

| Aqua Golf | 501 W. Florida Avenue | Denver |

Driving Range and Par 3:

Greenway Park	110 Greenway Drive	Broomfield
Twilight Golf	1090 S. Quebec	Denver
Mountain View	5091 S. Quebec	Denver

Public Golf Course and Driving Ranges:
(Listed in order of distance from Denver West Golf Range)

Meadows G.C.	6937 S. Simms	Littleton
Raccoon Creek G.C.	7301 W. Bowles	Littleton
Indian Tree G.C.	7555 Wadsworth	Arvada
Lake Arbor	8600 Wadsworth	Arvada
Hyland Hills	9650 N. Sheridan	Westminister
South Suburban	7900 S. Colorado	Littleton
Arrowhead G.C.	18050 Sundown Trail	Littleton

Private Golf Courses and Driving Ranges:
(Listed in order of distance from Denver West Golf Range)

Rolling Hills C.C.	W. 32nd St.	Golden
Hiwan C.C.	30671 Clubhouse Rd.	Evergreen
Lakewood C.C.	W. 10th and Pierce	Lakewood
Bear Creek C.C. (men only)	12201 Morrison Road	Denver
Willow Springs C.C.	16235 W. Belleview	Morrison

Miniature Golf:

Putt-Putt	4311 Wadsworth	Wheat Ridge
Putt-Putt	10480 Ralston Road	Arvada
Putters Park	9670 W. Coal Mine	Littleton
Mountain View	1876 S. Quebec St.	Denver
Putt-Putt	1520 W. 72nd Ave.	Arvada
Sportsglenn	2225 E. 10th Ave.	Northglenn
Putt-Putt	2270 S. Federal	Denver

Situation Analysis Worksheets

The worksheets provide a guide for developing various sections of a marketing plan. The following sheets cover situation analysis, including economic climate demographic factors, demand trends, technological trends, competitor analysis, and a SWOT analysis. Complete these worksheets as a preparatory step in the creation of a marketing plan.

Analyze the current economic climate in your region.

_____

_____

_____

_____

_____

_____

_____

_____

_____

Investigate the legal issues that apply to your industry segment.

_____

_____

_____

_____

_____

_____

_____

_____

_____

_____

List specific demographic factors pertinent to marketing your product.

_____

_____

_____

_____
_____
_____
_____
_____
_____
_____

Investigate the demand trends that apply to your industry segment.

_____
_____
_____
_____
_____
_____
_____
_____
_____
_____
_____

Describe how factors associated with the Product Life Cycle would affect marketing your product.

_____
_____
_____
_____
_____
_____
_____
_____
_____
_____

Site the technological trends that will affect your marketing plan.

_____
_____
_____
_____
_____
_____
_____
_____
_____
_____

Complete competitor analyses for the most immediate competitors in your market.

Competitor #1

Product Characteristics

Strengths

Weaknesses

Opportunities

Threats

Current Market Share

Current Actions in the Market

Probable response to your actions

_____
_____
_____
_____
_____
_____

Competitor #2

Product Characteristics

Strengths

Weaknesses

Opportunities

Threats

Current Market Share

Current Actions in the Market

Probable response to your actions

_____
_____
_____
_____
_____
_____

Other Competitors

_____
_____
_____
_____

_____

_____

_____

_____

_____

_____

_____

_____

_____

Analyze the internal status of the company (an internal SWOT).

_____

_____

_____

_____

_____

_____

_____

_____

_____

_____

_____

_____

Chapter Four

TARGET MARKETS

Markets and Consumers

Differentiation between a market and a consumer may appear, on the surface, to be trite. Kotler and Armstrong (2006, p. 7) defined a market as "the set of actual and potential buyers of a product or service." However, it is necessary for sport marketers to obtain both "macro" and "micro" perspectives. The macro perspective can give you an overall view of the group to which your products or services will be provided. This includes wholesalers, retailers, and eventual purchasers. In marketing terms, this macro approach includes "the mass market." The micro view examines each specific consumer of the product or service. This concept could lead to what is referred to as one-to-one marketing. Somewhere in the middle is niche marketing. Niche marketing is a term that refers to identifying and developing a relatively small, but discernible, market segment and attempting to capture a large portion of that segment. A comprehensive discussion about consumers, consumer analysis, markets, target markets, and market segmentation can be found in *Fundamentals of Sport Marketing* (Pitts & Stotlar, 2007).

In identifying groups of consumers, be careful not to jump to the conclusion that the purchaser and the user are the same people. Many successful marketers have found that, while American children do purchase products directly, they also influence their parents' purchase of a specific brand of sporting goods totaling $300 billion per year for kids 10–19 years old in 2003 (Burke, 2003). Any situation where the ultimate user is not the same person who makes the purchasing decision puts the marketer in a position of deciding whom to target for market communication.

Many scholars have researched consumers in an attempt to determine what actually happens in the decision to purchase. Do kids purchase athletic shoes based on performance? First, know that 80% of athletic shoes are never worn for sport. Second, know that style is tremendously more important than function for kids. As their analyses became more refined, company executives began to encourage marketing psychologists to develop measures to determine the effects of different components on buying behavior. The work of psychologists in constructing, testing, and analyzing purchasing behavior theory has always lagged behind the analysis of social behavior, which is involved in buying most products. Similarly, reliable theory has yet to be authoritatively established for the sport industry. It is an immense challenge for us to understand why consumers do what they do. Market managers have long had to face the dilemma of the "black box" in assessing consumer behavior. The "black box" theory simply states that many variables are directed toward the consumer but only one output can be seen—buying behavior (McCarthy & Perreault, 1990).

In the black box concept, all of the marketing elements involved with a particular product or service are presented to the market, with consumer response as the only recognizable output. This response could entail either buying the product or service or avoiding the product or service. What exactly happens in the mind of the consumers is often a mystery. The key for sport marketers is to recognize that the consumer considers many variables and each variable is significant and perceived differently by various consumers.

A classic story repeated in so many marketing classes relates to the invention of a new mousetrap. It has been postulated that if you invented a better mousetrap, the world would beat a path to your door (attributed to Ralph Waldo Emerson). Now, to view this from a marketer's perspective, several questions should arise in relation to consumers:

1   Do the customers really have mice?
2. Do they need to be convinced that they might have mice?
3. Does it really matter?
4. If they do have mice, do they want to get rid of them?
5. Do they want to use a trap to catch them?
6. Would they rather have you do it for them?

Clearly, the question of what to do about a mouse problem evokes significantly different perspectives that can affect marketers. The more you know about your consumers, the better able you will be to match their needs with your products and

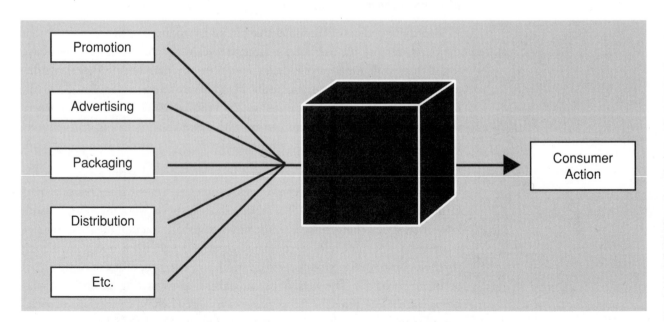

Figure 4.1. The Black Box Concept

services. Finding out who possible consumers are and how they behave is critical to sport marketers.

Determining Market Size

In idealistic terms, the possible market for any product includes the over 275 million residents of the US or, even more idealistically, the world population. But, in all seriousness, the potential market is composed of those people who have an interest in a product or service, adequate resources to purchase, and the willingness to relinquish those resources to buy the product.

Market size can also be measured in relation to its potential. As many coaches have said, "Potential is a heavy burden." So is the measurement of potential in a marketing plan. Using the data collected in the situation analysis (Chapter 3), forecasts can be made concerning the growth of the market, the number of people who comprise the market, and the demand trends in a particular product or service area. For more generic information, consult the U.S. Industrial Outlook published by the U.S. Department of Commerce/Industry and Trade Association. This can be ordered directly from the government on its website or found in most public libraries.

Marketing Research

All sport manufacturers and many sport organizations conduct market research. This is often based on a marketing information system (MIS). The topic of market research is presented in *Fundamentals of Sport Marketing* (Pitts & Stotlar, 2007), which provides a comprehensive discussion of research methods. Rodin (1998, p. 34) advises, "Research, and then research some more. Leave your office and talk to your customers. Quantitative, qualitative, and anecdotal research will provide unanticipated insights into what your product stands for and what your audience is hungry for." Some ski industry analysts collect their data skiing and talking to people on the slopes and chair lifts. While this technique is still practiced by some equipment manufacturers, many resorts are taking a more technologically advanced approach. By scanning a Universal Product Code (UPC) on a skier's lift ticket, the resort managers can track not only where the skier purchased their ticket and its price, but they can also track where the skier traveled during the day across the mountain.

These data provide valuable marketing information. The resorts are able to more accurately assess their promotional programs by tabulating the number of discounted tickets sold. This will also provide feedback on the distribution outlets in an easy-to-use format. Tracking the skier's activity on the hill can reveal the type of skier (beginner, intermediate, or advanced) using the resort. Furthermore, these data can graph traffic flow on the mountain as it relates to time of day and specific volume in different areas. Collectively, these data would be extremely valuable to marketing mangers at the resort.

While the collection of marketing data seems to be the intent of most MIS applications, an interesting use of the data occurred in 1998. Two teenagers skiing at Vail ski area in Colorado were reported missing after their day of skiing. Search and rescue teams examined MIS data in an effort to locate the last ski lift used by the skiers (season pass holders). The boys had skied in an out-of-bounds area, and the search and rescue personnel used scanner data to locate the last lift they used. This tactic helped the search parties confine their efforts in the area where the boys had the greatest probability of being found. Unfortunately, only one of the two boys survived the ordeal, but county deputies cited ski pass data as a primary factor in locating the survivor (Miller, 1998).

According to several researchers (Pitts & Stotlar, 2007; Mullin, Hardy, & Sutton, 2007), marketing research is vital for sports organizations because their fans, clients, participants, and consumers change rapidly. In addition, an MIS can enhance a quality control system by providing valuable information to be used in redesigning products and services. When using an MIS for decision making, remember that the quality of one's decisions is reflective of the quality of the information upon which they were based. Again, the topic of MIS is covered more thoroughly in *Fundamentals of Sport Marketing* (Pitts & Stotlar, 2007).

Grey & Skildum-Reid (2007, p. 23) ask, "So how do you get all of that information about your target markets so that you can create the strongest possible marketing plan?" The two main sources of MIS data are typically identified as being either primary or secondary. Primary research is conducted directly with customers, either by the firm or through contracted marketing experts. Grey and Skildum-Reid believe that this primary research is the best information. They provide an extensive list of methods that can be employed for collecting consumer information. These include ticket sales, contests, trial offers, coupons, registrations, point-of-sale material, Internet sites, kid pages, fans clubs, sales receipts, membership programs, warrantees, surveys, and product registrations (2007, pp. 163–164).

Sports organizations can, through a database, keep very accurate records of all their clients. This includes accounts payable and accounts receivable. Business schools teach the "80/20" principle (Stevens et al., 1997). This refers to the fact that, for many businesses, 80% of their business comes from the top 20% of their customers. For instance, in the golf industry, an examination of the number of days played by various segments of golfers may indicate that only about 20% could be classified as avid golfers (playing 25 or more days per year); yet if you were to examine the percentage of the total rounds of golf accounted for by these players, it would most likely explain about 80% of all rounds played.

PRIMARY RESEARCH

Many sports organizations generate data through client questionnaires or surveys. These can be valuable sources of information about customers' consumption of products and services, as well as short-term demand trends. One of the nation's leading sporting goods retailers, The Sports Authority, found that it had very little information on its customers. For years, they had assumed that most of their customers were men and had targeted their marketing efforts toward men. After posting losses during a period of expansion, the company engaged in market research through credit card data and online surveys, building a database across their 400 stores. What they found was that "women aged 25 to 45 contributed 70 cents of every dollar at Sports Authority, whether the purchase was footwear, fishing equipment, or Little League gear" (Coffey, 2002, p. 372).

The use of surveys and interviews has numerous advantages (Grey & Sklidum-Reid, 2007). As inexpensive research tools, they are extremely flexible, have the ability to reach a wide sector of your market, and can build a valuable database. Disadvantages include the dependence on the willingness of others to help and the difficulty in preparing a survey that will provide valid and reliable information.

The first step in conducting survey research is selecting the style and method of survey required. Which method will provide the best information in the least amount of time and for the lowest cost? The most popular methods for sports organizations are online surveys and personal interviews.

Direct Surveys

Direct surveys can be the basis of your information-gathering process or a supplement to other methods. This method entails presenting questionnaires through the mail or via an online survey site in order to collect opinions on a topic under investigation. If the sample group is small, a questionnaire can be sent to every member; if it is large, it is best to use the online survey or select a representative sample from the group (Grey & Skildum, 2007).

Typically accompanying the questionnaire is a letter explaining the survey's purpose and requesting the respondent to answer and return the questionnaire in an enclosed postage-paid envelope. If an organization has a postal permit number, they should use this on their return envelopes. This is more cost effective than affixing a stamp to the return envelopes because the organization is charged only for the questionnaires that are actually mailed rather than having to purchase the stamps (or run them through a postal meter) for the entire mailing. For online surveys, the respondent simply clicks "submit" when finished.

Sutton (1996) has been actively involved with primary research collection for a variety of professional teams. In one interesting investigation, Sutton worked with the Philadelphia 76ers of the NBA to assess customer profiles. While this practice is not atypical, this particular research was aimed at consumers who were not at 76er games. Sutton conjectured that the 76ers could learn more about marketing the team by investigating consumers in the general community. Indeed, they discovered that only 11% of the respondents thought that the 76ers were a better entertainment value than other teams in the city. The research also discovered that people did not think that the 76ers were active in community relations. As a result, the 76ers were able to adjust their marketing strategies and public relations activities to better meet their customers' expectations (Sutton, 1996).

Personal Interviews or Focus Groups

Marketing information sought in a face-to-face session between consumers and sport organizations characterize personal interviewing or *focus group research*. This method of data collection is well suited for complex products or services requiring extensive explanations or those that may be unfamiliar to the consumer. When more than one person is interviewed, the method is termed *focus group research*. Focus groups should include 10–18 people (Grey & Skildum, 2007). The interviewer usually has a questionnaire as a guide, but this is not normally presented to the interviewee(s). In order to accurately analyze the information received, a tape recording of the interview is often employed.

The popularity of this method is evidenced by the following advantages:

1. Responses are easily recorded.
2. Greater control can be obtained.
3. More detailed information can be gathered (Mullin et al., 2007).
4. A higher percentage of completed answers is usually achieved.
5. More in-depth questions and follow-up questions can be asked.
6. Personal contact often stimulates greater cooperation from the respondents.

Some negative attributes also accompany the use of personal interviews and focus groups as a means of gathering marketing information:

1. It can be more costly than other methods because of the wages involved.
2. Interviewer bias can distort results if adequate training is not done.
3. It is time consuming for both the interviewer and the interviewee.
4. Recording answers may make the respondent nervous.

Primary research can also take the form of pilot testing and product experiments. Those companies that manufacture sporting goods are continuously involved in this type of research, specifically in product development (discussed in Chapter 6). Because few other sports organizations engage heavily in these types of research, little time is devoted to this research activity.

Sport organizations are also consumers, and therefore, every supplier to the organization should also be considered a potential consumer. Many sport organizations purchase a wide variety of products and services each year. This could range from fertilizer for the field to hot dogs for the concession stand. These companies certainly have an interest in your continued success, and they may even feel an obligation to your organization. These companies could be contacted for ticket purchases, product donations, and sponsorship opportunities.

There are other ways of obtaining market research. Because many sport organizations do not have qualified analysts, a professional firm is sometimes hired to do the job. Turnkey Sports and Entertainment, the leader in the industry, offers full-service quantitative and qualitative solutions such as on-site intercept surveys and lead generation; focus groups; in-depth interviews; telephone, mail, and online surveys; online panel access; secret shopper programs; and as economic impact and feasibility studies (http://www.turnkeyse.com/Intelligence.html). This can also be a cost-saving measure because the analysis is often done only a few times per year, and hiring from outside vendors produces savings in personnel expenses. One of the main concerns regarding outside consultants is confidentiality. This is a major concern and should be a prerequisite to the release of any sensitive marketing data. Most of these firms can conduct the analysis and present the data; however, it is up to you to interpret the information as it relates to your marketing decisions.

SECONDARY RESEARCH

Secondary research is characterized by the fact that it is not conducted directly by the organization or its agents. Secondary research does not entail the analysis of an organization's own customers, but rather samples larger segments of the general market (Grey & Skildum, 2007). Several major companies are in the business of sport market research and provide valuable secondary sources of market information. A considerable amount of data can be obtained from this research by organizations that conduct and publish data for entire industries.

Mediamark Research and Intelligence (MRI) and American Sports Data are two of the more popular firms that produce marketing research relating to the sport and fitness industry. MRI provides demographics, lifestyle statistics, product usage data, and advertising media preferences from a wide sample of US citizens. Sections of data that may be of interest to sport marketers include data on sports participation, attendance, and equipment purchases (http://www.mediamark.com/). American Sports Data (http://www.americansportsdata.com/) presents its findings in one comprehensive volume (*Superstudy of Sport Participation*). However, concentrated, narrowly defined data reports can be purchased separately. Each of these resources details the consumer by such factors as age, income, geographical location, occupation, education, marital status, and size of family. The *Superstudy of Sport Participation* reports data for children as young as six years old, while MRI data begins at age 18.

Various details regarding attendees at sporting events can also be gleaned from the *Superstudy*. For example, if you wanted to know how many people in an average college basketball crowd earn over $60,000 per year, you could find a report that would show the amount is around 33.9%. Other types of available information relate to the average amount of money spent on sporting goods each year, the percentage of people who own their own snow skis, and the place where these items were purchased.

Following is another example of secondary research and trend analysis. The Sporting Goods Manufactures Association reported trends in US participation with some "hot" areas and some areas of decline (SGMA, 2007, p. 3).

- **Uno.** With more than 100 million overall participants (of which 70 million are core participants), walking for fitness is the #1 fitness activity.
- **Court King.** With nearly 15 million participants, tennis is the top racquet sport, and it's a top-ten activity at the high school level.
- **Women's Prerogative.** Of the 21 fitness activities listed, women account for at least half of the participants in 14 of them.
- **High Finance.** The sport with the highest average annual household income ($95,700) per participant is scuba diving.
- **Out.** Nearly 43 million Americans were members of health clubs in 2006, which is up from nearly 21 million in 1990.
- **One, Two, Three.** The three most popular team sports in the US—based on core participation—are basketball, baseball, and outdoor soccer.

- **Newcomers Welcome.** Lacrosse had the highest percentage of first-time participants, as nearly 40% of all participants were new to the sport in 2006.
- **The Home Front.** Wholesale sales of home fitness equipment in the US are strong, growing from $2.44 billion in '96 to $3.54 billion in '06.

The International Health, Racquet & Sportclub Association (IHRSA) is also a great source for information in the health and fitness industry (see also http://www.ihrsa.org). It conducts a thorough analysis of the fitness and exercise club industry and publish its data annually, which is available to both members and non-members. One of its publications is the "State of the Industry Report," a 100+ page study designed to help clubs correctly position their products and services. A sample of the type of data that it collects is presented in the Best Practice section of this chapter.

Stotlar and Johnson (1989) conducted market research for several major university football and basketball programs. The results of their investigations produced some interesting data for the sport administrators and are of special significance to corporations wishing to advertise in college football and basketball stadiums. The results of their demographic data indicated that the distribution of age and income for the fans at selected games closely matched national statistics for attendance at college sporting events, according to the Simmons Market Research Bureau. This showed the universities that, indeed, their audience was typical. It also demonstrated to potential sponsors that sports audiences are ones that many advertisers would like to reach. This, in itself, could assist those athletic administrators who wanted to utilize stadium advertising as an additional source of revenue.

The point of marketing research and data analysis is to better identify segments of the market that are most likely to purchase your goods and services. This necessitates what is referred to as *market segmentation*.

Market Segmentation

Markets consist of consumers, and each consumer differs from another. These differences can be used to view consumers as belonging to groups with similar characteristics. Market segmentation can be defined as "dividing a market into distinct groups of buyers who have distinct needs, characteristics, or behavior, and who might require separate products or marketing mixes" (Kotler & Armstrong, 2006, p. 47). "One of the most critical aspects of sport marketing is to segment the market of sport consumers into smaller homogeneous groups for which specific marketing strategies can be developed" (Kwon & Armstrong, 2004, p. 101).

In classic market segmentation, marketers often classify buyers by factors such as age, gender, occupation, income, attitudes, and geographic location (or any combination) and build a profile of those most willing and able to purchase the products and services offered (Fullerton, 2007). Pitts and Stotlar (2007) provide significantly more detail about this process in *Fundamentals of Sport Marketing*.

This concept is really an abstract or artificial view of the market. People don't normally form groups and live together in the same locale and view identical forms of media. They are interspersed in the community randomly, and our attempt at identifying them is based on our desire to direct marketing activities that they may find appealing. In the 1990s, most sport organizations looked at varied markets and attempted to identify segments of those markets that could be accessed. According to Gray (1991, p. 318), "Future market share will be won by the sport organizations that do a better job of identifying and targeting different market segments." One term used to describe the continued fragmentation of existing markets is *particle marketing*. This term further emphasizes the notion that sport marketers continually narrow their target market to meet the needs of ever-smaller segments of the market. Another term that can be applied to this phenomenon is *precision marketing*. Zabib and Brebach (2004) describe precision marketing as the "precise adjustment of product or marketing effort to consumer or user requirements" (p. 31).

Simply because a large market can be divided by these characteristics does not necessarily mean that it should. If a market has both female and male customers, there is no need to segment the market by gender if the two groups do not exhibit different needs or purchasing behaviors. Stevens et al. (1997) indicated that, ultimately, each buyer could be considered a specific segment (so called one-to-one marketing). While most manufacturers are not willing to customize a product or service for each individual consumer, this situation has recently started to change. There is a trend in many US industries to undertake more individualized product delivery. The most notable example is in the computer industry where Dell computers began offering custom designed/manufactured computers directly to customers from the factory. Several other companies quickly followed Dell's lead. The sport industry is also following this trend. Golf equipment manufacturers will produce clubs with an infinite array of shaft materials and flex ratings, club head materials and designs, as well as grip specifications. Where these choices were once only available through golf pro shops, they are currently available from many mail order and online suppliers at reasonable prices. Similarly, consumers can go to Nike's website and order custom-designed shoes.

Race is a factor to which many sport organizations are especially sensitive. According to Armstrong (1998, pp. 12–13), "There may be instances where undifferentiated (mass marketing) strategy may appeal to black consumers in the same manner as it may appeal to other consumers. On the other hand, there are also instances in which marketing strategies should be differentiated with a special appeal to black consumers." Marketing research has demonstrated that black consumers display some meaningful differences from other consumers. They have been found to be more brand loyal, prefer high quality merchandise, spend a higher portion of income on consumer goods, are status conscious, and are more willing to investigate new products (Armstrong, 1998). Thus, these consumers represent a market segment that would be attractive to many sport enterprises. Armstrong suggests several strategies that sport marketers should employ when targeting black consumers (Armstrong, 1998, pp. 13–15):

1. Hire professionals who have expertise with the black consumer market.

2. Involve the black media.

3. Employ a culturally based approach of marketing communication.

4. Engage in activities that allow blacks to identify with the organization.

5. Patronize black vendors.

6. Offer product extensions or amenities that have some salience to black culture.

7. Demonstrate concern and respect for the black community and causes salient to it through socially responsible/cause-related marketing.

8. Identify appropriate distribution channels to reach black consumers.

9. Invest in black youth.

10. Identify influential people from the black community to compose a support network.

There are some events that specifically cater to black consumers. The Bayou Classic football game is one. Staged in Louisiana for the last 30 years, this event pits two historically black institutions against each other in a three-day celebration of black culture and football. The event draws 70,000 people, and the game is almost upstaged by the half-time battle of the bands. As a sponsor, DaimlerChrysler saw the potential of predominately black audiences when they sponsored 32 historically black colleges and universities. Collectively, the schools have an alumni base of more than 15 million with an average income over $65,000. DaimlerChrysler got access to their databases and an on-campus presence during athletic events. Executives said, "It's a good audience for us, it's a professional audience of people who buy vehicles" (Lee, 2003, p. 18). Armstrong cautions sport marketers that minority consumers should not be viewed as a homogeneous segment. Similar to other definable segments, minority consumers display the same variances as other groups with regard to income, age, education, interests, and opinions.

Broad categorization can oversimplify a population. With Hispanic markets, the NBA office in Miami employs marketers from Cuba, Panama, Brazil, Argentina, Peru, and Puerto Rico. Similarly, the Asian community in San Francisco is made up of citizens of Koreans, Chinese, and Japanese descent (Brenner, 2004).

As American society continues into the 21st century, population demographics will continue to change dramatically with regard to race. It has been projected that by 2010 people of Hispanic origin will account for 13% of the population and by 2050 the percentage of Hispanic citizen will rise to 25% of the US population (McCarthy & Stillman, 1998). In 2004, Hispanics outnumbered African Americans for the first time, while Asian Americans rose to 4% of the population. (Brenner, 2004). With this data in mind, sport marketers have increasingly focused on the Hispanic market segment. These sport marketers are seeking new and innovative ways to attract this market to their products and services. In the product area, Gatorade developed and released a sub brand called Xtremo in 2002, targeted predominantly to Hispanic consumers in the Sun Belt. Using flavors already available in many Latin American countries, these drinks instantly captured a 2.5% market share. Numerous service examples also illustrate the trend. Several Major League Baseball teams have developed strategies to attract Hispanic fans. All most all MLB teams reported having radio flagship stations that broadcast in Spanish, six provided in-stadium informational signage in Spanish, and four major league stadiums contained advertising in Spanish. The Texas Rangers produced and distributed 75,000 fan guides and pocket schedules in Spanish. The Houston Astros moved to capitalize on their demographic situation by offering stadium tours in Spanish. Another indicator of the future can be seen where both Fox Sports and ESPN have cable offerings that broadcast exclusively in Spanish. It is also important to serve the fans once you attract them to the facility. Pro Player Stadium in Miami added media noche (a Cuban cheese and pork sandwich) and arepa (fried mozzarella on cornmeal pancakes) to their concession menu (Stern, 1993).

Spanish-language television stations are also playing an important role in sport marketing. Univision, the leading Spanish-language broadcaster in the U.S., was able to attract more viewers for soccer's World Cup than was ESPN. A significant factor for sport organizations is that Univision reaches 95% of the nation's 8.4 million Hispanic households (Mullen, 1998; Hemingway, 2002).

Another example of this strategy can be seen in Colorado where the Copper Mountain ski area organizes an annual Ski Fiesta sponsored by the Hispanic Chamber of Commerce. Loveland ski area promotes a similar activity with its Fiesta Del Sol weekend to help make Hispanic skiers more comfortable at the resort. In addition to special activities, the resort increases the number of Spanish-speaking ski instructors. Given the fact that the Denver area has a Hispanic market equivalent to 20% of the population, many resorts recognize that this segment has the potential to provide greater growth than more traditional segments.

Recent studies have shown that a market segment based on race may perform differently than other segments. Armstrong (2004, p. 7) noted, "Game promotions influenced attendance decisions of African Americans and Hispanics more than those of Asian and Caucasians." The sports marketer should give particular attention to the needs of all groups, and race may well be a factor that has not been effectively examined.

Similarly, examining customers by income categories may help marketers identify potential customers. Data show that only 35% of people with incomes of less than $15,000 exercised on a regular basis. Yet, when looking at those with incomes in excess of $50,000, more than 50% were regularly engaged in exercise programs. This data would certainly be valuable to marketers of fitness products and services.

Age is also an important factor to consider as a variable by which to view consumers. Many ski areas are increasingly looking to older skiers as a meaningful segment of the total market. Demographics in the US show that for the next 20 years one baby boomer turns 50 every 7.5 seconds (Milner, 2003). "They ski more days per year, spend more money at resorts and buy more second homes . . . Vail resorts called the 50-plus skiers 'an attractive marketing target' because of their sheer numbers and purchasing power" (Parker, 1998, p. 1L).

Cohen (1995) noted that, "Everyone takes a different view of the over-50 market, but one fact stands out in black and white—it's the future of the fitness industry" (p. 31). There are a variety of aspects of over-50 clients that appeal to the health and fitness industry. The 55+ age group represents 22.5 % of the total fitness market (35% of all health club memberships) and has increased 379% in the last 15 years (Lauer, 2006). This trend has also worked to redefine "old." Only a few years ago, "50 was old and 60 was dead" (Lauer, 2006, p. 150). These customers have the disposable income to spend on services, they are more concerned with health in general, and they typically have more time to devote to fitness-related activities than their younger counterparts. Lauer (2006) also predicted that "by 2050 all able-bodied people will exercise. Those who do not will be outcasts" (Lauer, 2006, p. 67). With the aging of the American population, age will undoubtedly surface as a significant factor in a variety of sport marketing strategies. The extensive numbers of these customers must be considered, and the trend will continue for the next 15 years (Lauer, 2006).

On the other end of the spectrum, younger consumers also offer an important segment of the market. SMGA data also showed that nearly 40% of all sports apparel spending is for clothing worn by children aged 17 and under (SGMA, 2004). Stoufer (1998) indicates that the Generation Y group (10–24 years of age) represents 78 million people (three times the size of the once valued Gen X) and spends $91.5 billion dollars per year. In addition, they influence an additional $246 billion in spending. From 1997–2005, this segment will grow by 18%. The trends indicate these consumers are interested more in participation than spectating and tend to focus on individual rather than team sports (Stoufer, 1998).

Sexual orientation is another demographic factor segmentation variable worthy of attention. Sporting events such as the Gay Games have become tremendously successful. In its first year, 1982, the Gay Games attracted over 1,300 participants and 50 spectators. The 2006 event in Chicago drew over 12,500 participants from more than 70 different countries, demonstrating that targeting events to specific demographic groups is a viable marketing tactic. Targeting gay and lesbian consumers has also proven to be an effective tactic for consumer goods. Research has shown that gay and lesbian consumers have higher product loyalty than other consumer groups (Pitts & Stotlar, 2007).

According to Kenneth, Sneath, and Erdmann (1997), "A purely demographic approach to segmentation has proven problematic to marketers in the past" (p. 56). Furthermore, Mullin, Hardy, and Sutton (2007) suggest that multifarious categories be utilized in the segmentation process. They propose classification according to "state of being" (demographics [including age, gender, income, education, family status], geographic location); "state of mind" (lifestyles, attitudes); and "product usage" (frequency).

Kwon and Armstrong (2004, p. 101) suggest, "Sport marketing research has not adequately addressed the complexity of psychographic factors that may influence marketing practices such as segmentation." Demographics define "what" your consumers are, whereas psychographics define "who" they are. Skildum-Reid (2007, p. 8) provided several questions that marketers should address in determining a target market's psychographic character.

1. What does my target market care about?

2. What are the sports or products that contribute to their self-definition?

3. What are the ways my target market consumes (at the stadium, sports bar, on TV)?

4. What about the sport experience is most important to my target market?

In general, psychographics include attitudes, interest, and opinions.

This breakdown of classifications will allow the use of multiple factors in designing market segments. Sports marketers are most successful when they use a multiple segmentation approach (Gray, 1991). Decisions must now be made on which market segments to address or target; hence, the concept of target markets.

Target Markets

Using Mullin's category of product usage, a marketer can classify users as heavy users, medium users, light users, defectors, and media consumers (Mullin et al., 2007; Kotler & Armstrong, 2006). Heavy users are those that consume the product or service on a regular basis. This would include season ticket holders, club members, and other frequent users. Medium users would consist of those who purchase the product on a less frequent basis. Some colleges and universities use mini-season ticket plans or promote group ticket plans. Some golf courses have weekday plans that are offered at a rate lower than full play memberships. These would be examples of light or medium users (Mullin, Hardy, & Sutton, 2007). Although many sport research companies use arbitrary numbers to segment groups into the various usage groups, you can use a formula driven by the segment's consumption rate divided by average consumption rate. Media consumers in sport are characterized by the fact that they only follow the team on television, radio, and in print. This can be due to several factors. The Denver Broncos football team had a history of selling out Mile High Stadium with over 90% of tickets sold to season ticket holders, corporate sponsors, or set aside for NFL or team use. Consequently, for years many fans were forced to support the team exclusively through the media outlets. In the mid-1990s, the Broncos began aggressive campaigns to attract these "media" fans in anticipation of a new stadium. In 1998, the voters of Denver approved the construction of a new stadium, and the next generation of fans responded with season ticket orders for the increased pool of tickets (the Super Bowl victories of the team during the 1998 through 1999 seasons also helped).

Some colleges and universities such as the University of Nebraska have been in similar situations, depending heavily on media consumers. Similarly, the Chicago Cubs and the Atlanta Braves of Major League Baseball have developed a nationwide following through the media, primarily because of specific television stations' use of satellite and cable technology. Sport marketers must remember that these people are consumers too and must be treated well and have their special needs addressed.

This geographical separation from consumers was addressed by the National Basketball Association (NBA) beginning in 1989. That year, more than 50 foreign countries televised NBA games. That number grew to 212 countries for the 2004–2005 season. More than 250 million people around the world participate in organized basketball programs. In fact, 42% of the traffic to the NBA's website is international. Based on this situation, the NBA expanded its coverage of 11,700 hours of television broadcasts in 42 languages. As a result of those efforts, 8 out of 10 international teens could recognize the NBA logo (Brockinton, 1999; Mullin et. al., 2007).

The success of this approach has not gone unnoticed by the major manufacturers in basketball either. Nike, Reebok, and Spalding all conducted marketing and advertising campaigns to coincide with this market. Internationally, Spalding and Reebok (now owned by adidas) sold over $20 million per year in licensed NBA merchandise, with Nike selling over $75 million in basketball shoes per year in the international market. The timing component was also important to the success of these programs. Basketball was on a steady rise in participation with several successful Olympic Games concluded for both men's and women's competitions.

Target markets can also be examined for profitability. One evening I was visiting with a prominent sport marketing guru and surprised where our conversation went. He told me that he had had an argument with his credit card company about a billing issue, and he stated emphatically that he was one of their best customers, noting, "I charge over $10,000 per month with you and always pay off my balance on time." It occurred to me that he was not one of the best customers but in fact one of their worst. They spent all of their resources servicing his accounts, generated airline miles for his account, and floated him a $10,000 loan every month and made $0.00 in the process.

In the previously cited situation in which heavy consumers consisted of season ticket holders, marketers must ask the question if season ticket holders are, on a per capita basis, the most "profitable" customers. It may be that because these consumers attend many games and receive complimentary parking passes as a part of their package, they may spend less per game than medium usage consumers. At some point, it may be wise to maintain the heavy users but concentrate on increasing the medium user and their revenues from parking, concession, and souvenir sales.

Benefit Segmentation

Just as consumers differ in where they live, how much money they make, and how often they buy, they also differ in their objectives in purchasing the product or service. Because marketing can be defined as the provision of goods and services that meet consumer needs, the unique benefits of a product or service that motivates a consumer to purchase must be examined. This is labeled as benefit segmentation.

As mentioned in Chapter 2, many sport products are intangible. For instance, we cannot assume that just because a person came to a volleyball game, he or she came to see the volleyball match. They may have come for the food, to be with a date, or just to support a friend on the team. Similarly, people buy running shoes for reasons of function, style, support, or safety. The important point to remember is that consumers buy products for different benefits associated with the purchase.

The ski industry provides a couple of examples in the area of benefit segmentation. There are only about five major manufacturers of ski bindings in the world, and each offers a line of various bindings. But what are the benefits of each model? Some buyers want the top of the line competition model. Why? Is it because they see themselves entering the Olympic Games in the downhill? No, it may well be that they just want to say that they have competition bindings. It could also be that they generally buy top of the line products, simply because they can afford it.

Another purchaser may be in the market for skis where a considerable array of choices is presented. The desired specifications include performance, handling, durability, and style. Sports marketers (and of course sales staff) must be able to determine the benefits desired by individual customers. In some markets, promoting a ski because the World Cup champion used it may be a great strategy, while in other markets style may be the key to success. Shaped skis became the rage in the late 1990s, even though some skiers could not detect any measurable difference on the snow. People just wanted to have the most advanced look for their skis. These people were making choices of skis based on their parka color. Similarly, most Americans would rather buy a less expensive ski parka in the latest color, despite that it is not of the highest quality material, whereas most Europeans would rather buy a parka with conservative style and more durability.

Database Marketing

A natural confluence between the concepts of Marketing Information Systems and market segmentation is marked by *database marketing*. Database marketing is grounded in the belief that market planning begins by understanding the customer—his or her buying and consumption patterns, location, interest, and other aspects of buying behavior. Although database marketing has been widely and successfully used in the domain of business operations, its application in sport is still in its infancy (Fielitz & Scott, 2003). Mullin, Hardy, and Sutton (2007, p. 92) noted that such "data are especially crucial for sport organizations because fan and participant trends appear to change so rapidly." Zabin and Brebach outlined the basic process in developing a customer database. First, you need to "capture and mange customer data," then you need to "analyze the data to derive strategic insights," and then "use those insights to drive more efficient and profitable customer interactions" (2004, p. 65). They indicated that such a database would enable the organization to easily identify their best customers, reinforce purchasing decisions, conduct marketing research, and increase marketing efficiency.

Following the process noted by Zabin and Brebach, the initial step in building a consumer database is the collection of information from or about consumers. Many corporations use product warranty cards to start the process. On many warranty cards, consumers are requested to respond to a variety of demographic and lifestyle questions. These data become the essential components of the company's database. Other frequently used methods for collecting data include business reply activities, coupons, and sweepstakes. Many sport organization have found success with fan club members or others signing up in their database by offering people who "opt in" first-in-line privileges on team promotions and special deals.

Two sport-related examples can provide some direction. Spoelstra (1997) explained the situation with the New Jersey Nets of the NBA. When he began directing the marketing activities of the Nets, he was amazed that the ticket office had few records of previous season ticket purchasers. Much of their sales were conducted through Ticketmaster. Ticketmaster would purge their files at the end of the basketball season. Spoelstra had Ticketmaster retrieve their backup files to start building the database for the Nets. In addition, the Nets needed to amend the way they handled information requests. Previously, if a person called to request a team schedule, the office personnel would listen on the telephone and print the caller's information directly on an envelope (time saving, no doubt) and then mail the schedule out to the caller. Spoelstra saw this as "throwing away" potential customers. As a result, he revised the office practices to ensure that data on callers was entered into the computer prior to the requested schedule being mailed. Thus, the Nets were able to capture more potential customers.

Another example of database building comes from the New Jersey Devils of the NHL. As part of their sales systems, as with most professional sports teams, the Devils engaged in a variety of group sales activities. However, the data derived from group sales was very different from the data that Spoelstra was building in the example illustrated above. In group sales, you would only get the name and address of the group leader or organization. The individual names and addresses were not typically available. However, the Devils came up with a method to acquire this valuable data. They would have one of the players autograph a hockey stick and have the group members complete raffle cards for a chance to win the autographed stick. Thus, the Devils were able to collect data on people who they knew were already interested in attending hockey games and treat them as potential season ticket buyers. A similar tactic was used by Kroenke Sports and Entertainment (owners of the Colorado Avalanche [NHL], Denver Nuggets [NBA], Colorado Rapids [MLS]). This company held an online sweepstakes with the prospect of wining an autographed Colorado Avalanche jersey, an effort that produced over 15,000 email addresses of prospective customers. The same activity with the Nuggets yielded 9,000 email addresses for the database (Migala, 2005).

Other research by Chen, Stotlar, and Lin (2007) with the Denver Nuggets showed that by analyzing customers' past ticket purchase behavior professional sport organizations could effectively predict a customer's next ticket purchase. This research showed that data mining/database marketing was possible and feasible within the professional sport segment of the sport industry.

The use of database marketing in recreational sports has also proven successful. Handel (1997) stated the objectives for using database marketing as (a) the retention of current customers, (b) the recognition of which segments generate the most business, and (c) the recruitment of new customers. He cited one specific example where the use of a database resulted in an 11% increase in participation. This was accomplished by using the database to contact previous participants and inquire about their interest in upcoming programs. Additional information about database marketing will be presented in Chapter 6 on marketing strategies.

It is possible to create your own database software for marketing; however, at the onset, you may be better served by purchasing one of the commercially available software packages for database marketing. Mullin, Hardy, and Sutton (2007) found that the expansion of basic customer data, such as demographics, psychographics, and product usage, can result in a Customer Relationship Management (CRM) System. The CRM system could "capture the number of season tickets a fan purchased, the seating location, and all of the payment data" (Mullin et al., 2007, p. 96). The advances in CRM are such that an estimated $12 billion dollars is spent annually on software, hardware, and system maintenance.

Identifying, targeting, and communicating with a particular segment of a market is only one aspect of the process. You must get the consumer to actually exchange his or her money for your product or service.

Consumer Behavior

The black box theory described earlier indicated that we know very little about what happens in the mind of the consumer, but as portrayed above, we can collect data and learn more about them. A significant amount of research exists regarding consumer behavior and motivation in sport. The parameters of this book preclude a full discussion of the factors. However, some attention is warranted. Sport consumers have been classified into two distinct groups, direct and indirect. Direct consumers purchase sport products or attend sports events in person. Indirect consumers consist of spectators at sporting events. Of course, both groups are important to sport marketers.

Mullin et al. (2007) classified purchasers according to one of the following approaches to consumer behavior:

1. **Economic.** This view of consumer behavior looks at the ideal concept, in which the consumer makes objective purchases based on logic and facts. We all know that these people are out there, but not everyone falls into this category. Those who ascribe to this view believe that if you put a good product in front of consumers for a reasonable price, they will buy it.

2. **Psychological.** This approach examines consumer attitude and its effect as a predictor of behavior. However, it is important to note that there may be a difference between the intent to purchase and what is actually purchased.

3. **Sociological.** This approach dentifies social influences such as demographics, parental influence, and peer group pressure. These, of course, differ with each consumer or market segment.

4. **Behavioral.** This concept forwards the notion that everything is a result of interaction with the environment, rather than a stimulus and response. The ultimate intent is a change in behavior.

Mullin, Hardy, and Sutton (2007) further noted that sport consumers are influenced by a multitude of other factors. These include cultural norms, commitment to sport, stage in life cycle, ethnicity, and other personal and environmental factors. A multitude of studies have examined the motivations of consumers for attending and watching sports events. These motivations have been classified as empathy (feelings about the team), social integration (enjoying the game with friends), team effort (players do their best), team affiliations (connectedness and strength of identity), achievement (winning), entertainment (fun factor), skill (watching high level performances), drama (unpredictability), and escape (forget troubles) (James & Ross, 2004). The research has shown that all of these factors play important but varied roles in consumers' decisions to attend sporting events. Marketers should give particular attend to the variables as they apply to their unique sport setting.

Another approach to the individual consumer is the identification and classification of buyers in terms of readiness to purchase and adopt a new product (Kotler

& Armstrong, 2006). Pride and Ferrell (2008), among others, indicate that buyers move though specific stages prior to making a purchase. This process is highlighted by the following table.

We also know that not all purchasing decisions are the same, and as such, not all consumers complete all of the steps in the decision process. Consumers are more highly involved in complex and expensive purchases (a competition touring bicycle) and less highly involved in more simple and inexpensive purchase decisions (golf tees). Therefore, although both consumers recognize the need for a product, the person seeking golf tees would engage less in gathering information and evaluating alternatives than would the bicycle purchaser. The level of brand loyalty also enters this equation because, for some products, previous experience with a particular brand decreases the consumer's quest for alternatives. So, you can see why all sport marketers are interested in developing brand loyalty.

Kotler and Armstrong (2006) noted that consumer purchasing behavior can also be examined by their readiness to try new products. They classified the consumer groups as Innovators (2.5% of consumers), Early Adopters (13.5%), Early Majority (34%), Late Majority (34%), and Laggards (16%). Kim and Stotlar (2007) found that a classification of golf club consumers along this construct showed that golf consumers fell into only three clusters, Early Adopters (34.6 %), Early Majority (25.4%), Late Majority (39.9%). Their research also found that consumers were most likely to seek information about new golf clubs first from print media and second by word-of-mouth from other golfers. Finally, as one might expect, the early adopters had lower handicaps and higher income than other groups. How a corporation can move customers though this process is many times a function of marketing strategies, as discussed in Chapter 6.

The consumer's personal psychological makeup is also a vital aspect in understanding consumer behavior. In marketing, these psychological aspects are normally referred to as *psychographics* or *lifestyle characteristics*. These characteristics relate to the consumer's activities (hobbies, club affiliations, vacations, social entertainment); interests (media, community, family); and opinions (about self and others, regarding products and services in the market). According to Gray (1991), sport marketing authorities refer to these measurements as activities, interests, and opinions (AIOs).

McCarthy and Perreault (1990, p. 178) provided a variety of factors that could be examined in an analysis of AIO.

Table 4.1. Consumer Purchase Decision-Making Process

- **Identification of the Need**

Example: The consumer comes to the realization that s/he needs to begin to engage in an exercise program to regain some perceptible level of fitness.

- **Quest for Information**

Example: The person begins a quest for information on health and fitness clubs in the immediate area.

- **Evaluation of Product Alternatives**

Example: Once information is collected about the various clubs, the consumer must make some decisions concerning which club offers the most appropriate programs and amenities at the best price.

- **Purchase of the Product**

Example: After evaluating all alternatives surrounding personal criteria, the consumer finalizes his/her selection by signing a membership contract with the selected fitness center.

- **Post-Purchase Satisfaction**

Example: Once participate in the programs of the fitness center begins, the consumer starts to reevaluate the purchase decision, using the criteria on which the selection decision was made. This results either in a confirmation of satisfaction or dissatisfaction regarding the purchase decision.

Table 4.2. Activities, Interests, and Opinion Factors

Activities	Interests	Opinions
Work	Family	Themselves
Hobbies	Home	Social Issues
Social Events	Job	Politics
Vacation	Community	Business
Entertainment	Recreation	Culture

(Adopted from McCarthy and Perreault, 1990)

"Even though measuring and analyzing the consumer's lifestyle can benefit marketing, the sport marketer should be aware that the consumer's subjectivity and tendency to report desired behavior rather than actual behavior can make psychographic qualities difficult to measure" (Gray, 1991, p. 317). The scope of this text does not allow for an in-depth review of this concept, but you should consider examining Icek Ajzen's *Theory of Planned Behavior*.

The psychological process for online or Internet purchasing is somewhat different than for on-site retail consumers. Zhang and Won (2004) noted that the biggest challenge for Internet marketers is the creation of trust. Because, in contrast to buying in a store, online purchasers cannot touch the merchandise to assess its quality, trust in the quality as transferred from the seller becomes critical to the transaction. Several aspects of trust were found to influence the consumer's purchase intention. First, if the product were a known brand, trust would be high even if the seller were less well known. Secondly, if the consumer has had previous positive transactions with the specific online retailer, then trust is higher. Finally, some consumers are more likely to trust based on their personality and life experience than are others. As an important element in purchasing, trust can also be transferred from friends and family who have had experiences with a seller or product. So collectively, if high levels of trust can be developed, online retailers can enhance their chances for success (Zhang & Won, 2004). Because trust can also be transferred from others and has been shown to be an important component in the decision to purchase, marketers should examine the influence of opinion leaders.

OPINION LEADERS

Opinion leaders are individuals who have greater levels of product knowledge and can influence consumer groups. They usually consider themselves to be "experts in the field." The use of opinion leaders in sport marketing is not a new concept. Athletes have been used to provide product endorsements for many years. It has been postulated that their endorsements will result in increased sales, yet data regarding the effectiveness is mixed. On the other hand, some believe that this component of sport marketing can be effective when matched to target markets and applied appropriately with consumers in different stages of buying readiness.

One of the more successful developments in this area is the extensive expansion of a product line in consort with an individual player. The example of the relationship between Nike shoes and basketball player Michael Jordan demonstrates the extent to which the concept can evolve. Few authorities would question the impact that Jordan's endorsement has had on Nike sales. Reebok has used a more direct application to retail sales in sporting goods stores. Many Reebok representatives would "seed" a market by giving away pairs of their newest shoes to some of the young sales associates in the stores. While no agreements were made for the sales person to push Reebok shoes, most wore the shoes and developed favorable opinions about the company as a result.

All of the major shoe companies also use coaches as opinion leaders. This really gets to the "grass roots" of the market. Some college coaches have been paid as much as $1,000,000 per year to outfit their team in Nike shoes. The exposure achieved through this endeavor comes not only in the arena but from the television coverage of the games as well. Consider the economic value of a game televised nationally for three hours to millions of viewers. Even high school coaches can be involved in similar programs. Although few receive cash contracts from shoe companies, many will get free shoes and clothing for their coaching staff and T-shirts for their summer camps. Any coach of an organized sports team can, with a little effort, become involved in a discount program. Many programs grant their teams the right to purchase shoes from a retailer at a reduced cost.

Several companies have high school programs that supplant discounts offered by local retailers. These companies typically require a minimum purchase of 15 shoes, give a 15% discount, free practice shirts for players, and a free pair of shoes for the coach. The same marketing theory prevails; if a high school team is wearing a particular brand of shoes, the younger kids will want to wear them, too. And besides, the younger kids grow out of them faster and then need to buy another pair! Therefore, Reebok's $1.5 million sponsorship deal with the California Interscholastic Federation was easily justified.

In an effort to attract buyers in large groups, some sporting goods manufactures have sought endorsement from the National Federation of State High School Associations (NFHS). Nine companies had "approved" volleyballs, 2 had footballs on the list, 5 soccer balls were cited, as well as 26 different basketballs (14 models from Wilson alone). Through this association with the NFHS, companies hope to influence sales of the "approved" models and gain significant market share over their competitors.

Other ways of using opinion leaders in sport have included soliciting their opinion. This can be valuable as a source of information for the organization and also makes the individual feel influential. Many sports teams use this method with their season ticket holders. Questionnaires are sent to them requesting their opinions on everything from team uniforms to concession food.

Product sampling and prototype testing are additional ways to receive input from opinion leaders. This too makes them feel that their opinion is important, and it can provide the company with reliable feedback on products for very little cost. This strategy has worked well for snowboard manufacturer Burton. They "put a real premium on having athletes on our team that can test product, help us develop product, and at the same time, show people what the product is capable of doing" (Rofé, 1998, p. 28)

The use of opinion leaders in marketing campaigns must be executed with care. In particular, if you are "attempting to reach Generation Y, [they] don't want to be sold . . . so soft-selling is the key" (Kovatch, 1998, p. 21). When K2 wanted to market its in-line skates, they set their advertising budget at zero. The idea was to do what they termed "in-the-market marketing" by using end users (authentic endorsements) or enhancing relationships directly with retailers (Kovatch, 1998,

p. 21; see also the Best Practice section of Chapter 6). These activities brought K2 more credibility than could have occurred with a more traditional use of marketing dollars.

The marketing process must now shift from an analysis mode to a stage of greater action. Within the framework of your organization, you must now choose which of these segments will be most productive, when the best time is to reach that particular segment, and where and how they can be reached. This entails setting market objectives and selecting strategy.

BEST PRACTICE

Presented below are data showing secondary data available from the International Health, Racquet & Sportsclub Association retrieved March 28, 2008, from http://cms.ihrsa.org/index.cfm?fuseaction=Page.viewPage&pageId=19362&nodeID=15

BOSTON—March 17, 2008—The International Health, Racquet & Sportsclub Association (IHRSA) announced today that early estimates from an annual tracking study indicate health club membership in the United States increased by three percent last year, from 42.7 million members (over the age of six) in 2006 to 44.1 million in 2007, while industry revenues increased by 5% to $18.5 billion. This growth in health club membership represents an increase of more than 115% in ten years, while growth in total revenues represents an increase of 127%.

Data reported in IHRSA's annual membership report, Profiles of Success 2007, indicate that clubs have also improved upon membership retention from 2005 to 2006 by three-percentage points, increasing from 70% to 73%. Simultaneously, participating IHRSA clubs raised total revenue per member by nearly 5.5% in 2006 to $741.80.

"As an industry, we aim to grow total membership year after year, and industry stability is in no small part dependent on customer satisfaction, membership retention, and increasing revenues per member," said Joe Moore, President & CEO of IHRSA. "The dedication to customer service demonstrated by IHRSA members is clearly evident as this data shows an increase in total membership and member retention. IHRSA health club operators across the nation are providing their members with desirable and essential services–an essential component to running a high-quality business," said Moore.

The typical club surveyed in regards to non-dues revenue reported generating nearly one-third (32.1%) of total revenues from internal profit centers. "These profit centers provide evidence of the clubs' ability to develop programs and services that meet consumers' fitness and recreation needs," said Katie Rollauer, IHRSA's Senior Manager of Research.

Additional results found that clubs' steady improvements in revenue growth (5.4% over 2005) and membership growth (4.2% over 2005) contributed to an overall improvement in productivity and profitability. Specifically, the typical business responding to the survey reported a 6.6% increase in the revenue per square foot ($53.50), while club profitability for the entire sample improved by better than three percentage points to 11.3% (pre-tax earnings a percentage of revenues) in 2006. "These observations reflect a club's ability to control costs while generating overall growth," said Rollauer.

http://cms.ihrsa.org/index.cfm?fuseaction=Page.viewPage&pageId=19362&nodeID=15

U.S. HEALTH CLUB MEMBERSHIP DATA

The following information represents a sample of findings from current and past IHRSA research. Additional historical data, more complete findings, and current statistics can be found in the annual Profiles of Success, available in PDF format in IHRSA's online bookstore (http://www.ihrsastore.com). To purchase, call 800.228.4772 or 617.951.0055.

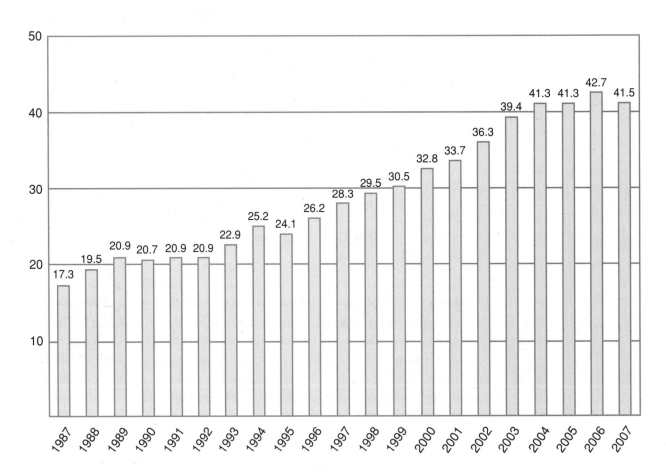

Figure 4.2. U.S. Health Club Growth (Million)

Survey results represent membership number for a broad range of facilities, including park and recreation centers, hospital fitness centers, YMCAs, college and university centers, and commercial clubs.

Source: 2005 IHRSA/American Sports Data Health Club Trend Report

Target Market Worksheets

The worksheets provide a guide for you in developing various sections of your marketing plan. The following sheets cover target marketing, including marketing information systems, available primary and secondary data, market segmentation, target markets, benefit segmentation, buyer readiness, consumer lifestyles, and opinion leaders. Complete these worksheets as a preparatory step in the creation of your marketing plan.

Describe the marketing information systems that will be most valuable in gathering data for detecting your target market.

_____

_____

_____

_____

_____

_____

_____

_____

_____

Investigate and list available sources and methods for gathering primary data.

_____

_____

_____

_____

_____

_____

_____

_____

_____

Search and record available sources for secondary market data.

_____

_____

_____

_____

_____

_____

_____

_____

_____

Determine which factors will be critical for segmentation for your market.

_____

_____

_____

_____

_____

_____

_____

_____

_____

Identify specific target segments within your markets with a rationale for their selection.

_____

_____

_____

_____

_____

_____

_____

_____

_____

Detail specific product benefits that you will use to segment your consumers.

_____

_____

_____

_____

_____

_____

_____

_____

_____

Assess the process in which your buyers engage in purchase decision-making.

_____

_____

_____

_____

_____
_____
_____
_____
_____
_____

Stipulate consumer lifestyles that will be included in your target market.

_____
_____
_____
_____
_____
_____
_____
_____
_____
_____

Identify possible opinion leaders that could be used in your marketing strategies.

_____
_____
_____
_____
_____
_____
_____
_____
_____

Chapter Five

MARKETING OBJECTIVES

Setting Marketing Objectives

Once the management team has defined the organization's mission, completed a situation analysis, and identified a target market, specific marketing objectives need to be established. They provide, in essence, that "road map" or "game plan" to the overall corporate mission. Managing by the marketing objectives set is also critical. In one example, the athletic director at St. Louis University told the sports marketing assistant to "put a lot of time and effort into women's sports." However, he noted that the year-end evaluation would be based on attendance at men's basketball games. This is not the recommended approach.

Many authors have used the acronym SMART to craft marketing objectives. SMART stands for Specific, Measurable, Achievable, Results-oriented, and Time-bounded (Grey & Skildum, 2007). This acronym is easy to propose but difficult to operationalize. It has been noted that "marketing is one of the least understood, least measurable functions at many companies" (Farris, Bendle, Pfeifer & Reibstein, 2006, p. XV). More specifically, Grey and Skildum (2007, pp. 141–142) described how objectives could be written in the SMART format.

1. Rather than stating "Increase Sales" as an objective, you should write: "Create incremental sales of 10% during the six-week promotional period as defined by retail orders."

2. Instead of "Develop Database," the objective could read: "Develop a database of no fewer than 2,500 prospects as determined by your target market profile."

3. Stating "Gain Publicity" as an objective could be rewritten as, "Gain a minimum of 10 high level and 15 medium level publicity placements during the first quarter of the year."

4. "Demonstrate Good Corporate Citizenship" could be stated as, "Increase favorable public opinion of the company from 45% positive to 55% positive over the first 2 quarters and measured by the company's satisfaction survey."

The establishment of these marketing objectives will ultimately serve as management's control system for the marketing process. This system is essential in achieving the objectives and for correcting any deviations from the marketing plan. A basic principle of control is that you don't control costs, schedules, or performance standards, you control the people who are responsible for those elements. You do this by making people directly accountable for specific results. Therefore, your objectives must be people-specific, while at the same time results-oriented.

The first step in the process is to establish the marketing concept around which you will base the objectives. The basis of the marketing concept is to establish a competitive differential advantage. Cohen (1998, p. 36) notes, "You must direct your efforts toward satisfying the customer by achieving a competitive differential advantage over your competitors." Thus, your marketing objectives should be communicated in terms that clarify your intended competitive differential advantage as well as specified levels of sales and profit.

Objectives are often developed around the concepts of quantity and quality. Do you want more customers? Do you want different customers? Do you want better products or services? Do you want to sell more of the existing products or services? These present you with quantity and quality choices. More is not always better, and better is not always more profitable.

Athletic departments may not want more athletes; they may want better athletes. The novice sports marketer may want to achieve both; however, they may, at times, be mutually exclusive. In order to entice more athletes, additional financial aid may need to be offered, but this may negatively affect the department's profit margin.

In another sport situation, would you rather sell 10,000 tickets at $2.00 each or 1,000 at $20.00 each? Can you make more money by selling fewer tickets at a higher price or by selling more tickets cheaper? Some promoters are interested in "putting cheeks in the seats" while others look solely at the revenue generated. Much of this will be discussed in the next chapter on marketing strategy.

Marketing objectives must be quantified and qualified. How good is good? How many is more? Your objectives need to be written in directional terms with specific levels of achievement. You should avoid using such terms as better, more, and higher, as these are too subjective and difficult to measure. Psychology also supports the notion that people are more committed to goals and tasks that appear in written form. As an example, the marketing objectives generated by a sport medicine center have been provided at the conclusion of this chapter in the best practice section. They are written, specific, and measurable.

The succeeding step in constructing effective marketing objectives is to assign a particular individual or department the accountability for their accomplishment. Most experts on management would agree that individuals would be more motivated to work toward objectives if they have played a part in their development. This may involve participative management techniques such as a Total Quality Management (TQM) approach, Management by Objectives, or another familiar form of organizational management. Although this is often a function of management style, it would be advantageous to discuss specific objectives assigned with the person to whom they are to be delegated. A face-to-face exchange is often necessary to assure the person clearly understands the objective.

From a management perspective, it must also be remembered that the objective assigned must be within the control of the person to whom it was given. For example, to require that a sports information director increase the number of column inches that appear in a newspaper is not within his or her control. You could, however, require that the number of press releases produced by the department and submitted to newspapers be increased a designated amount.

After the objective is written and assigned, a timeframe must be developed for its completion. There is no general rule for the length of time for any task. It should fall within the rule of reason. What is reasonable for one objective may not be reasonable for another, and what a supervisor and employee consider reasonable may also vary significantly.

Some mangers have suggested time frames of one year. It should be noted that a danger exists in setting timeframes without checkpoints. Can you afford to go to the end of the year and find that an objective was not met or met to a 50% level? As a consequence, you may want to set yearly objectives and require quarterly reports, and then, changes in either assignments or personnel can be made before the organization is too adversely affected. The evaluation process will be discussed further in other chapters.

There is no scientific formula to assess whether the right objectives have been chosen. That is why the process must be one of constant evaluation and monitoring of the situational factors upon which the objectives were set. However, the marketer must not lose sight of sustaining a competitive differential advantage through the accomplishment of their objectives. Again, Cohen (1998, p. 36) states, "Why should anyone buy from us as opposed to our competitors?"

Activation constitutes the last step in the process. In a real sense, this is the development of marketing strategy. What must a marketer do to make the objectives work? The subsequent chapter is devoted to this process.

BEST PRACTICE

DENVER BRONCO'S SPORT MEDICINE CENTER

Sustaining Marketing Activities

The Denver Bronco's Sport Medicine program offers complete care for injured athletes participating at any level of competition. Three freestanding centers and a soon to be fourth center offer state-of-the-art equipment and staff specifically trained in sport medicine diagnosis and rehabilitation. Each center faces regional competition from local hospitals, PT Centers, and other sports medicine programs. The Denver Bronco's Sport Medicine program faces competition from individual physicians and the Challenge Center.

Centers are developing a premier reputation through the use of the Bronco's name, word-of-mouth endorsements because of their successful treatment programs, and work with coaches and schools. Successful implementation of the following marketing objectives is dependent on staff support and the operational budget.

MARKETING OBJECTIVES

1. Support referral relationships
   - 65% of new patient base from physician referral
   - 31% referral from previous contact with staff or prior patients
   - Remainder from special event marketing activities

Budgeted—$4,000

2. Sustain media support for free injury evaluation program
   - 100% increase in use of service
   - 15% of free injury evaluation referrals from physicians
   - 50% client generation from evaluations

Budgeted—$29,000

3. Target new market of sport participants aged 12–17 (market share and size currently undetermined)

Budgeted—$34,000

4. Conduct market segmentation analysis to compete with
   - Humana's target of female competitive athlete market
   - Swedish's target of skier injury market

Budgeted—$4,000

5. Sustain Special Events/Promotional Activities
   - Denver Nuggets Sponsorship at $49,000
   - Coaching Clinics at $3,000
   - Open House Activities at $1,000

Budgeted—$53,000

* Author's Note: This example does not provide an assignment of personnel directly to the accomplishment of these objectives. Also, from an analysis perspective, one may want to examine the cost efficiency of the Denver Nuggets Sponsorship activity based on the number of clients and revenue generated.

Marketing Objectives Worksheets

The worksheets provide a guide for you in developing various sections of a marketing plan. The following sheets cover marketing objectives, including responsibilities for accomplishing the proposed time frame for completion, creating an evaluation system, and assigning the required human and financial resources. Complete these worksheets as a preparatory step in the creation of a marketing plan.

Specify five or six marketing objectives for your sport entity.

_____

_____

_____

_____
_____
_____
_____
_____
_____
_____

Assign specific responsibilities for the accomplishment of each objective.

_____
_____
_____
_____
_____
_____
_____
_____
_____
_____
_____

Develop a detailed time frame for the accomplishment of your marketing objectives.

_____
_____
_____
_____
_____
_____
_____
_____
_____
_____
_____

Describe the system that you will use to evaluate your progress toward accomplishing the objectives.

_____
_____
_____
_____
_____
_____
_____
_____
_____
_____
_____

Itemize the human and financial resources required to accomplish your marketing objectives.

_____

_____

_____

_____

_____

_____

_____

_____

_____

_____

Chapter Six

MARKETING STRATEGIES

Strategic Marketing

According to Stevens, Loudon, Wrenn, and Warren (1997, p. 26), "In most planning scenarios, strategy follows objectives." Marketing strategy consists of the complete plan for the accomplishment of the organization's mission and stated objectives. Hiebing and Cooper (2003, p. 108) observed, "Marketing strategy is a statement detailing how an individual marketing objective will be achieved. It describes the method for accomplishing the objective." Strategy defines the exact procedures for this linking process, providing an action plan. In the previous chapter, tasks were developed and assigned to members of the staff. Thus, the method by which those tasks are accomplished is determined by the marketing strategy selected.

Traditional Market Strategies

Strategic market management is a system designed to help you make decisions regarding a fit between your organization's goals and resources and changing market opportunities (Gray, 1991). McDonald and Keegan (2003), Kotler and Armstrong (2006), and Brooks (1990) suggest four alternative market strategies: new market penetration, market expansion, product development, and diversification. These are not mutually exclusive and can be conducted simultaneously. Each, however, has its own unique processes and outcomes. Pitts and Stotlar (2007) provide significantly more detail about this process in the *Fundamentals of Sport Marketing*. The following pages present an overview of strategic market management and an application of the basic approach for the fitness industry as delineated by Brooks (1990).

NEW MARKET PENETRATION

Entering the market constitutes that first and scariest step in actually infiltrating the business world. Ries and Trout (1986), in their definitive work on positioning, have suggested that being first in the market has the distinct advantage of securing a firm place in the mind of the consumer. Being first also provides valuable experience in manufacturing and allows sales representatives to attract customers before the competition arrives. However, not everyone can be first. If you are not first in the market, you need to establish a market position.

In positioning, you are attempting to gain a well-defined place in the mind of the consumer. Kotler and Armstrong (2006) indicated that positioning is "arranging for a product to occupy a clear, distinctive, and desirable place relative to competing products in the mind of the consumer" (p. 49). Even if an organization is first in the market, their strategy should be to shape the perception of their product or service. That perception may be based on a particular product performance characteristic, such as safety, comfort, or durability. It could be based directly on an advantage that an organization feels its product has over the competition.

Considerable work has been done in the area of positioning. The depth of the materials is beyond the scope of this book, but an overview is appropriate. Hiebing and Cooper (2003) recommend that position be determined by mapping critical elements of an organization's product or service against those of their competitors. This technique was briefly discussed in Chapter 3 regarding competitor analysis. The point is to distinguish your product from competing brands and develop a strategic advantage in the market (Kotler & Armstrong, 2006). A marketer can begin the process by identifying and listing product attributes that are important to customers. This could include quality, price, selection, fashion, and reputation, among others. Next, rank the attributes in order of importance from the consumer's standpoint. Then, evaluate product on a 1–10 scale and do the same for each competitor. This process, when mapped on a grid, will reveal gaps for product improvement and strategy definition. This necessitates some market research, but the data are important for proper strategy development.

Regardless of the attribute around which an organization chooses to form its "position," the goal is to shape and solidify that image in the consumer's mind and to separate offerings from those of competitors (Erch, 1998). This strategy drives many other aspects of marketing planning. Specifically, it affects promotional messages, advertising placement, and packaging, among others. These factors should provide significant advantages that would be difficult for late-entering competitors to overcome (Kotler & Armstrong, 2006).

While the advantages of entering a market first are clear, there are also latent dangers. One danger of being first at anything is that you are prone to mistakes. Mistakes are sometimes costly. If an error is made, an opportunity is presented for competitors. In sport, many times athletes talk about "going to school" on an opponent. This is the concept presented here. Competitors are quick to seize opportunities to capitalize on market opportunities. Take, for instance, the innovation of the oversized golf clubs. When Calaway introduced the Big Bertha driver, competitors quickly developed similar clubs, copying the design of the Calaway club, yet offering the product at a substantially lower price. Thus, some advantages also exist for late entry into markets. Extending the idea of learning from the mistakes of companies already in the market, late entrants can glean the best ideas and attack "soft spots" in the market.

According to Brooks (1990, p. 28), market penetration involves "attracting more participants to your established programs." Market penetration can take on two dimensions. An organization can pursue new markets with existing products or attempt to have existing consumers consume at a higher rate. Brooks (1990) provides an example of market penetration, stating that, for a fitness center, this would mean "1) attracting aerobic participants from another club or those who are using CDs at home, and 2) encouraging your present participants to increase their frequency and volume of purchases" (p. 28).

Another approach to getting existing consumers to buy in greater quantities was detailed by Mullin, Hardy, and Sutton (2007) in their Attendance/Participation Frequency Escalator. This model operates on the principle that it is easier and cheaper to get existing consumers to buy more than it is to attract new consumers. Gray (1991, p. 317) stated, "Sport marketers should realize the importance of classifying consumers by product usage. The differing needs of light, medium, and heavy consumers must be satisfied as much as possible." Having introduced the concept of "usage level" as a means of classifying sport consumers, this theory forwards the concept of moving consumers from the position of non-consumer to heavy consumers. Figure 6.1 illustrates the concept.

This strategy has been implemented by several major sports organizations, including both professional and college teams. The suggested methods for implementing this theory are as follows (Mullin, Hardy, & Sutton, 2007):

1. Unaware Non-consumer to Consumer—increase promotions and other communications. Encourage word-of-mouth recruiting. Utilize a "bring a friend" or "spread the word" type promotion.

2. Aware Non-consumer to Consumer—communicate product benefits and range of benefits.

3. Media Consumer to Consumer—media advertisements featuring benefits that can only be obtained on site. "Get the feeling" and "be a part of the action" have been popular themes in this method. Specifically, the ATP tour stop in Singapore used the slogan "Nothing Compares to Seeing It Live." Another successful method entails an emphasis on the "place" component of marketing. Many of the newly constructed baseball stadiums opted for a more nostalgic style to attract customers who had become disenfranchised with the "new era" of baseball.

4. Light to Medium Consumer—product giveaways, theme promotions, and contingent promotions have all been used as tools in this process. The most successful has been the contingent promotion. Here, fans fill out an entry

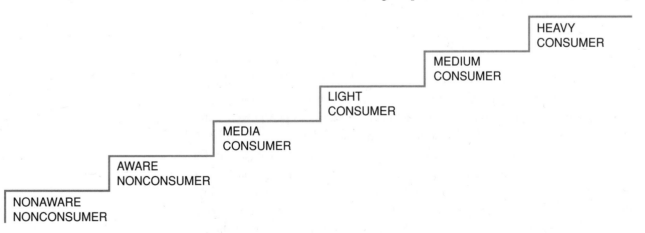

Figure 6.1. Mullin's Attendance/Participation Frequency Escalator

(Adopted from Mullin, Hardy, and Sutton, 2007)

blank that qualifies them for a prize drawing to be held at another contest. To win, they would be required to attend additional contests. Although giveaways (hat day, bat day, etc.) have been popular, there is conflicting research regarding whether they result in increased attendance. Data from NBA studies show almost no effect on game attendance; however, MLB data have indicated that increases as high as 20,000 people per game are attributable to such promotions. Theme promotions provide a vehicle to offer a product benefit other than the core and may successfully introduce spectators to the core product. One of the more successful promotions implements by several MLB teams in the late '90s was to giveaway a popular Bobble-Head toy. Not only did this provide an incentive for fans to attend, but it served the purpose of attracting younger fans for the sport (Fan promotions, 1998; Mullin et al., 2007).

5. Medium to Heavy Consumer—specific programs targeted for medium users often include mini-season, as opposed to full-season, ticket plans. These have been offered in split season (first half/last half) and in "Pick 10" (or 20, etc.) plans where fans select only certain games. The danger that exists for the split season plan is that many fans find the last half most desirable. In college sports, this usually reflects conference play, and in the pros, it is the title stretch. It may also cause an erosion of full season ticket holders. The NBA New Jersey Nets offered their "Pick 10" program in a mixed form with a forced choice of games from opponents with losing as well as winning records (Mullin, 2007). Similarly, the Baltimore Orioles offered successful packages with their Sunday afternoon games.

6. Maintaining Heavy Consumers—these people constitute the lifeblood of most sport organizations. The task, therefore, becomes one of rewarding consumer loyalty. This has traditionally been done through giving season ticket holders choice of the best seating and the first opportunity to upgrade. If the team in question qualifies for the playoffs, these consumers usually get the first chance to buy tickets. Other promotional methods have been targeted at heavy users such as special souvenirs, listing in programs, and even travel packages for away games (Mullin, 2007). Northwestern University created some special incentives for its season ticket holders by providing them with exclusive phone numbers to contact the athletic department, access to invitation only events, customized emails from the coaches and staff, and a personalized webpage (Boyer, 2003).

Mullin et al. (2007) discuss methods to reduce consumer attrition, a major problem for many fitness clubs and facilities. An example could involve a health club that tracks its members' participation records, which signals a response mechanism from the club. Members who had not participated for a week's period were automatically sent a note (through their computer's integrated database and word processing system) that said, "We miss you, hope to see you soon." Those absent for two weeks or more were sent a letter which said, "We still miss you—have a free drink on us next time you visit" (with a coupon enclosed) and, "Let us know if anything we have done is keeping you away." If the patron was inactive for three weeks or more, a telephone call was placed in order to determine the reasons for the absence. This amounts to what Fullerton (2007) called "recovery marketing." Aligning with what Mullin et al. (2007) suggested, Fullerton said that your contact should be personal and offer a value-added solution to the customer. Various studies have shown that it costs 5–6 times as much to attract a new customers as it does to keep an existing one.

Maintaining loyalty is accomplished in a variety of ways by different sport organizations. Traditionally, many organizations recognize milestones in membership or service. This can be done through awarding pins, patches, or the "Gold Watch" approach. One major ski resort in Austria gives special pins to return visitors, and several college booster clubs have color-coded decals to signify years of service. Mullin et al. (2007) explain that many sports fans would rather have more practical rewards for their support and detail examples where sports teams offer free game programs to those who renew their season tickets, escalating to free parking and free stadium club memberships for longstanding clients.

The best overall strategy for loyal customers lies in deepening the relationship. The Miami Heat (NBA) developed a "buddy program" where members of the Heat staff were assigned to contact season ticket holders several times during the season. Sometimes it was to notify the person of an upcoming event or just to ask if there was anything that the team could do for them. One Heat executive said, "There is nothing more important than our season ticket holders and it has brought our entire organization together to humanize this" (Migala, 2003). Chapter 7 also discusses this concept as it has been applied in professional sport through the advent of relationship marketing programs.

MARKET EXPANSION

In market expansion, an organization attempts to increase the volume of products sold to totally new consumers. This differs from the previous example in that an organization is not merely attempting to sell more products or services to existing consumers. Market expansion is achieved by getting a bigger share of the untapped (new) consumers to purchase your product or service, basically attracting a new market. If this is the intent, an organization must move more people along the purchase decision-making continuum presented in Chapter 4.

Perhaps an example will clarify this strategy. A British company, Allsport, was established primarily as an agency for sport photographers to market their pictures. Operating as a productive agency, with credits in many of the world's top sport publications, the agency has long been considered very successful. However, in finding new markets for their existing products, they proved to be even more successful. During the latter part of the 1990s, Allsport noticed that advertising and marketing firms were increasingly using sport images to sell their products. However, these "fashion models" had little experience with sports activities and often appeared awkward in sport settings. Therefore, Allsport began to market its photographs to advertising and marketing firms, creating new markets for their existing (and future) products (Roberts, 1997). An additional benefit from this tactic for many athletes was that doors were opened to commercial avenues in modeling and advertising, which might have otherwise been unavailable.

Another classic example is when the National Hot Rod Association (NHRA) introduced the Sport Compact Series. The NHRA was born in the 1951 from an effort to get young kids and their customized cars off the streets and into a safe racing environment. Identical motivations led to the NHRA's establishment of the Sport Compact Series in 2000. Thus, the NHRA was able to extend its existing product (drag racing) to a new market (today's young kids and their small import sports cars).

Market expansion is most often accomplished with either better or more promotions to ensure that the new market is informed about the product. According to Brooks (1990, p. 28), "Market expansion is not easily accomplished and usually requires more costly research to identify the size of the potential new markets and how much advertising and promotion will be required to attract this market." Promotions will be discussed in depth later in this chapter.

One final innovative example merits attention. The sales of tennis equipment paralleled the decline in participation during the late 1990s. Thus, many of the corporations that depended heavily on the tennis market began to look for other revenue sources. Penn Racquet Sports, one of the top retailers of tennis balls, found new customers in dog owners. Having noticed that dog owners used tennis balls to play "fetch" with their dogs, they created specially designed and packaged tennis balls in two-packs called "R. P. Fetchems" to serve this market. Priced at $4.00–$5.00 per two pack, the Fetchems produced considerably more profit than the tennis balls for humans, which sold for between $3.50 and $4.00 for a tube of three (Rofé, 1998).

PRODUCT DEVELOPMENT

An organization can also expand their market by creating new products and services to meet the needs of existing markets. These would be products or services of a similar nature that current customers (or those like them) would be interested in purchasing. For example, almost all the major shoe manufacturers have developed apparel lines to compliment their shoes. Later in this chapter more information about specific sports products and their related marketing aspects is given. The process of discovering/determining new products must be presented first.

Every new product/service begins as an idea. The process of generating ideas, evaluating them, and selecting the appropriate ones for development and marketing is complicated. A systematic approach to information gathering can be effective in new product development. The system should include a variety of input channels; this may be a complaint department where customers can respond to the products or services received, a suggestion box in which employees can forward new and interesting ideas in a non-threatening format, or a formalized group specifically assigned to develop and evaluate new product ideas. Several examples are discussed below.

Camp Woodward, a well-established summer camps for kids, began to offer new products through their camps in response to the changing desires of America's youth. They have BMX, skateboarding, and inline skating facilities, as well as instruction for beginners and coaching for the elite. Through a partnership with ESPN, they have also co-sponsored Junior X Games competitions.

The television industry was dependent on the regular schedule of college, amateur, and professional sporting events for many years. In the 1980s, they discovered they could also create sports products. One of the most successful examples is ESPN's X Games. This "made-for-TV" sport has served as a catalyst for similar programs in the television industry. In general, television networks are most interested in events through which they can establish an "equity" or ownership position.

The fitness industry, a bastion of the young and single for much of the 80s and 90s, responded to its customers' lifestyle changes (marrying and parenting) by instituting daycare facilities in many centers. Within a few years, this developed into children's fitness programs that became an integral product within the industry. American lifestyles, in which many families have two working parents, supported these programs principally to engage children in worthwhile after-school activities.

New ideas are often generated through brainstorming sessions. Questions that could be useful in this process:

1. What other products do our customers need?
2. What other uses might there be for similar products?
3. What other uses might there be for current company skills?
4. What adaptations could be made of current company technology?

Regardless of the source of the idea, the process should accept the idea without prejudgment. An evaluation system should then be implemented where each idea can be fully investigated.

Product development is generally referred to in terms of products or services that have never been introduced to any market. Entry into a new market has distinct advantages for a sport marketer. Being the first in a market always generates a considerable amount of interest by the consuming public and often results in free publicity. Another competitive advantage is gained because the experience of an initial entry is ahead of the competitor's. This often allows an organization to improve cost-efficiency before the competition, which in turn allows the use of resources for promotions while the competition's resources are being spent on development and production. This further entrenches an organization's hold on the market (Cohen, 1998). Momentum is a powerful force in sport marketing. Getting consumers to switch brands once their buying preference is established is a difficult task.

Disadvantages of early market introduction include the risk that buyers are unfamiliar with the product or service and are therefore reluctant to purchase. There is also the risk that the anticipated market never develops as forecast. Those who choose to take new products and enter the market later, rather than early, are able to gain insight from the experiments and lessons learned by pioneers. Experience is a good teacher, but many times it is also a costly one.

One example is Nike Inc.'s entry into the lightweight running shoe market. No other company chose to develop this type of product or was able to predict the expanding market. Experimenting in their basement, the founders developed a product called the waffle trainer that was a first in the industry. Although many competitors tried to overtake them, Nike has held a premier position in the running shoe market for decades.

DIVERSIFICATION

Diversification is characterized by creating new products for new clients. An interesting example of this can be found in a recent example. A leading football helmet manufacturer examined the unique characteristics of their products and technology and discovered that they had the capability of producing additional consumer products requiring impact-resistant plastics. Thus, they were able to increase their corporate profits by manufacturing cell phone cases for sale to cell phone assembly companies. With existing personnel, equipment, and technology, an entirely new product was launched and marketed to new clients. The high quality of their manufacturing produced a product that was far superior to others being made by traditional plastics companies at the time.

Historical examples also exist. The Hillerich and Bradsby Company, makers of Louisville Slugger baseball bats, engaged in similar product diversification. Their examination of their products, skills, and technology led them to other products, such as lawn mower rollers, gunstocks, and golf clubs (Pitts & Fielding, 1989).

More recently the Sandvik Corporation, a leading manufacturer of high quality steel products, applied its technological know-how to the construction of javelins in the 1970s. It soon became the best product on the market and one used exclusively by world record holders. The same mentality surfaced in the early 2000s when they began to manufacture and market bicycle frames. It shows how companies can use existing assets to produce new products for new markets.

Niche marketing, discussed earlier (Chapter 4), is the practice of identifying a small but definable segment of consumers for your product. As one colloquialism says, "Be a big fish in a small pond, as opposed to a small fish in a big pond." Moving Comfort, Inc. successfully accomplished this strategy. During the running revolution of the 1980s, many women found the running shorts they were wearing did not fit very well, basically because they were designed for men. Ellen Wessels saw opportunity within this context. Subsequently, she and a friend started Moving Comfort, which eventually generated about $12 million in annual sales of running apparel for women. Wessel successfully identified a niche market comprising 55 million female sport participants (Zavian, 1998). In the early 2000s, many of the outdoor equipment makers also began designing and manufacturing products designed specifically for women. Lackett (2003, p. G1) said, "The outdoor market has finally realized that there is an untapped potential here. The newer women-specific backpacks offer narrower shoulder straps with more pronounced curve and even a slightly cut out back panel to allow for the way women's arms swing." However, the profitability of this approach is limited, precisely by the factor that created the opportunity—market size.

In the 1980s, Nike set forward to move from its niche of providing shoes for elite performers to a more mass-market orientation. However, "Nike's push to satisfy the expanding mass market eroded its performance image" (Rudolph, 1989, p. 54).

Table 6.1. Strategic Opportunity Matrix

	Existing Products	New Products
Existing Markets	Market Penetration	Product Development
New Markets	Market Expansion	Diversification

By 1990, Nike had firmly refocused on its prior success. Nike executives said, "We make high performance basketball shoes for high performance players... We think what differentiates Nike from Reebok is performance positioning and the technology of our products" (Bagot, 1990, p. 62). Reebok's response in the 1990s was to accentuate their advances in technology (DMX) and refocus their advertising messages. Reebok introduced an advertising campaign based on "a running heritage and authenticity" (Rohm, 1997, p. 22). The stated mission was to establish a "true-to-the-sport performance image" (p. 18). Most notably, Reebok introduced an entirely new line of performance shoes in 1998, featuring newly developed technology. To reinforce their performance image in the 2000s, Reebok forged alliances with the NBA, the NFL, and MLB for on-field marketing rights.

In the final analysis, you can sell more things to the same people (market penetration), the same thing to different people (market share development), different things to the same people (new product development), and different things to different people (diversification). The matrix in Table 6.1 (modified from McDonald & Keegan, 2003, p. 42; Brooks, 1990, p. 29) shows how marketing strategy is patterned by each of these factors.

Brand Management

Kotler and Armstrong (2006, p. 243) define a brand as "a name, term, sign, symbol, or design or a combination of these intended to identify goods and services of one seller or group of sellers and to differentiate them from those of competitors." Although brands are typically associated with a product, branding and brand management for sport organizations should not be confined to a product brand. While brands originally functioned to identify and differentiate products, corporate branding can represent the unique attributes, meanings, and values that represent the corporation as a whole. "Understanding the meaning and value of the brand provides direction and purpose to everyone involved with the organization, gets them on the same page, and creates a culture around what is really important" (Brand Management, 2004, pp. 1, 4). According to VanAuken (2002, p. 1), "The brand embodies the heart and soul of the organization." This was emphasized by Kotler (2003, p. 11): "Your people must live out the brand spirit at the corporate level and the job-specific level. Thus, if your company brands itself as innovative, then you must hire, train, and reward people for being innovative. Once you define the attributes of your brand, you need to express them in every marketing activity." To illustrate brand management, excerpts from Nike's 2004–2006 brand plan are included in the Best Practice section at the end of the chapter.

The value of a brand is difficult to assess. However, with the bankruptcy of venerable sport companies like Converse and Top-Flite, the value of the brand was obvious. Nike was able to secure the Converse name for $305 million, giving it a platform to market lower priced and less technical shoes. Callaway secured the Top-Flite brand for more than $135 million to complement its own brand of golf balls with a less expensive alternative that already had market relevance.

The NCAA has recently been concerned with its brand image. Research about the public's perception of the NCAA centered on making money, not educating student-athletes. The NCAA wanted its enforcement activities to be seen as supporting "fair play." Unfortunately, the public viewed their activities negatively. Their target for 2006 was to have the public associate the organization "with learning, character, and fair play, instead of Final Fours and enforcement" (Brown, 2003, p. 3).

Sport enjoys a unique position in the marketing world. Bruce (2004) refers to the concept, *team as brand*. There are many brands to which consumers are loyal. However, the power of a sports team is unparalleled. I grew up near St. Louis, and the Cardinals are my team. I like BMW but not with the same passion that I like the Cardinals. The same can be said for university sports teams looking to build their brand. There are special connection between the fan and the school. These cannot be underestimated and must be nurtured. Every team executive wants more than just fans—they want "brand advocates" that will stay with the brand through the good times and the bad (Bruce, 2004). Perhaps the best way to comprehend the components of branding and brand development is to examine the IEG Brand Model (Brand Management, 2004, p. 4)

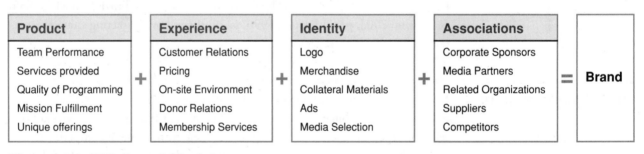

Figure 6.2. IEG Brand Model

Source: Adopted from Brand Management, 2004

Relationship Marketing

One of the buzzwords in marketing is "relationship marketing," the focus on interactions between the company and the consumer. In the 1990s, several scholars began to scrutinize the traditional marketing mix (Chapter 7) and the 4P approach to marketing. Their contention was that the increased complexity and sophistication of the consumer market had made traditional approaches to marketing ineffective and that a new approach was in order. Most notably, Grönroos (1994) called for a paradigm shift from the 4P approach of marketing to a relationship-based perspective. Although "relationship marketing is still in its infancy as a mainstream marketing concept" (Grönroos, 1994, p. 16), many authorities in the field have embraced it. Kotler and Armstrong (2006, p. 13) noted, "Customer relationship management (CRM) is perhaps the most important concept of modern marketing." Relationship marketing can be defined as "an integrated effort to identify, maintain, and build a network with individual consumers and to continually strengthen the network for the mutual benefit of both sides through interactive, individualized, and value-added contact over a long period of time" (Fullerton, 2007 p. 385). According to Kotler (2003, p. 151), "One of the things of most value to a company is its relationships—with customers, employees, suppliers, distributors, dealers, and retailers." In this sense, customers should be considered a valuable corporate asset just as much as production facilities or finances.

Relationship marketing came about primarily because of revolts against the invasive marketing practices that existed for centuries. Invasive marketing has been around for hundreds of years. Merchants displayed signs above their stores, identifying the type of products sold in the store. This provided information for the consumer and was seen as providing a benefit to customers looking for products and services. Newspaper advertising arrived in the early 1800s, and over two centuries, advertising has expanded though the mass media, progressing from radio to television, and now the Internet. However, many believe that traditional advertising has outlived its usefulness. Consumers are exposed to thousands of advertising messages each day. US data shows that the average person is exposed to 3,000 advertisements per day (Godin, 2000). The clutter has become so overwhelming that many believe advertising is ineffective. Do you pay attention to commercials? Do you "channel surf" during the commercials? Do you use TiVo and skip the commercials? What about banner ads and pop-ups on the Internet? To many, advertising has become meaningless "noise." The best method to effectively communicate with consumers is not by interrupting them, but rather obtaining their permission to pursue a relationship. Skildum-Reid (2007, p. 10) stated it most succinctly, commenting that event signage "was created to divert the audience from the experience they are trying to have. This is not good. If you want your brand to be an invited part of someone's life, there is no better way achieve that than to add value to their experience."

Because there are generally enough sport products and services to meet consumer needs, consumers are not motivated by advertising to explore new options. Therefore, sport marketers need to create a shift from focusing on near-term transactions and invasive marketing to establishing relationships and obtaining permission to contact customers. The primary issue has now become a question of how to create this relationship and obtain permission. McConnell and Huba (2004) note that sports teams should begin by gathering as much feedback from their fans as possible. Teams like the Dallas Mavericks, Portland Trailblazers, and the New Orleans Saints have established "fan advisory boards" for the purpose of gathering input.

In this respect, sport organizations have begun to explore alternate methods to communicate with consumers. Sport marketers often send press releases to the media. Why not add your fans to the distribution list? They will get the latest news, often before the general public. This makes them feel very special and increases their identification with the team. The U.S. Olympic Committee sends special notices to their club members with news stories and human-interest pieces on select athletes and sports. Many of these stories would never be published in the regular newspaper because they have limited interest. However, because these people have a special interest in Olympic sport, they enjoying receiving this information. The Phoenix Suns have also successfully used e-newsletters with their fans. During the 2005–06 season, they were able to solicit 110,000 subscribers (Migala, 2005).

Relationship marketing can provide two very important benefits. Mangers who implement relationship marketing techniques will become more knowledgeable about customers in general. This can assist the organization with product development and market assessment. A second benefit is purely economic. Estimates vary, but it is generally accepted that it costs at least five times as much to recruit a new customers as it does to maintain an existing one (Fullerton, 2007). Principally, loyal customers buy more products for a longer period of time than do occasional purchasers. The effect of retaining current customers is most apparent in the fitness industry. Current figures indicate that the attrition rate for fitness club members is about 54%. Thus, you could calculate that a club with 1200 members would lose 648 members in the course of one year. Therefore, the club would need to sell 54 new memberships per month to maintain their membership levels.

In professional sports, several organizations have implemented relationship marketing programs. Patterned after the airline industry's frequent flier programs, these schemes offer fans membership in a fan club, special incentives for repeat purchases, and exclusive offers on merchandise and other team services. The most successful programs have been the Compadres Club of the San Diego Padres and the two programs offered by Mighty Ducks of Anaheim and the Los Angles Angels of Anaheim. Started in 1995, the Padres enlisted 90,000 members by 1998, and their data indicated that 46% of members increased their attendance by 6.67 games over the 1997 season (please note that the Padres also appeared in the 1998 World Series). By 2002, that number had increased to 10.7 games over a season. The Seattle Mariners indicated that their 74,000 club members generated an additional $10 million in revenues. Pride and Ferrell (2008) noted that, because service marketing involves intangible assets, managing the consumer relationship becomes critical. Relationship marketing works particularly well in sports because the customers are more connected to the sport and teams than are non-sport consumers. Sport consumers demonstrate their loyalty by wearing team-related merchandise and in general have been involved with the team for a long period of time. According to Bee and Kahle (2006, p. 104), "Sport consumers that exhibit sports-loyalty behaviors, such as repeat purchasing and continued attendance, are the key to a sport organization's success."

All of the major professional teams have websites where fans can access team statistics and stories, but can they interact? Online forums and chat sessions have been found to be quite effective in building positive relationships with fans. They create just the "buzz" and "community" that McConnell and Huba (2004) propose as key elements in creating loyal fans. Similar to Mullin's escalator, this approach results in more loyal fans who consume at higher rates, become repeat customers with higher loyalty ratings, and are less price sensitive. Through relationship building, consumers can become involved with your sport organization as a partner, not just a customer. In many ways, these new marketing methods are similar to those of long ago. Get to know your customer, visit with your customer, and design products and services to meet their individual needs. If you insist on traditional techniques and interruption marketing, you will end up with former customers. Regardless of the label or designation assigned to the marketing program, relationship marketing or marketing mix, it is essential for your organization to carefully evaluate the market and customers in order to design programs that meet their needs.

Tribal Marketing

There are many marketers who believe that the days of segmenting and marketing to people on their demographic characteristics have passed, that building relationships is one-sided and simplistic, and that experience marketing is too shallow to have real meaning for today's sophisticated consumer. Tribal marketing gets its origins from the concept of "tribe" or "clan." Cova and Cova (2004) propose that tribal marketing differs from relationship marketing in that relationship marketing looks at creating a bond between the company or brand and the customer, whereas tribal marketing focuses on the connection between customers. They contend that relationship marketing confuses proximity and intimacy. In a 2004 advertising campaign, Verizon Wireless developed the "Are you in?" campaign, where the company served to link groups of people together. Tribes are created and survive on emotion, not cognitive clarity. In sport, we see numerous examples of "diehard" fans. The Cubs, the Red Sox, the Yankees, and the Dodgers, among others, all have loyal fan bases. They are connected by shared emotion and feelings. With the Internet, significant portions of our day are spent on the computer, without meaningful interpersonal interaction. We can obtain almost anything we want from the privacy of our homes. Theorists suggest that, in response to this phenomenon, people are desperately seeking meaning from their lives and Tribes can provide it. Cova and Cova (2004, p. 10) define a tribe as "a network of heterogeneous persons—in terms of age, sex, income, etc.—who are linked by a shared passion or emotion."

Snowboarders represent one of the more recent sport-related examples of a tribe. "Snowboarders represented a marginal group, a tribe, which structured itself against the whole universe of skiing (federations, clothes, brands . . .). They wanted to stay apart from traditional skiers. They had their own small manufactures (more than 150 craftsmen), their own distribution channels (Pro-Shops), [and] their cult brand (Burton)" (Cova & Cova, 2004, p. 18.). The Salomon brand was seen as an outsider, yet the company desperately wanted a share of the growing market. In the best practices section at the end of this chapter, there is an overview of Salomon's strategy and tactics.

All of the above strategies place a specific demand on available resources. The selection of an appropriate strategy should examine the extent to which resources are used. Resources may include personnel, finances available, and facilities (both production and distribution). For instance, an organization may have a research and development division that is not currently overburdened. This may, therefore, be the time to work on diversification. Yet, in this scenario, if working capital is a problem, it may not be the time to attempt to get the different products to new markets, but rather to confine the strategy to market expansion. In another situation, current programs may be doing well, but it is perceived that a greater market share could be gained through increased advertising and promotion. Here, market penetration should be pursued. Given the unique nature of sports and sports teams, relationship marketing and tribal marketing may shape your marketing strategies.

Through the selection and refinement of your marketing strategy, you are striving for a competitive advantage. Do you want to be a price leader, with good products offered at better price than your competitors? Would you rather be known for providing better service than your competitors? In some segments of the industry, the goal is to make your competitors irrelevant. As noted previously, the scope of this text does not allow for in-depth discussion of all possible marketing strategies, but this last point deserves some space.

Regardless of the strategy chosen, it is important to document and support the pursuit of any or all of the marketing strategies. Then, as the organization proceeds and environments change, managerial changes can more easily be made. The actual commercialization of sport requires an intricate management of the functions of marketing presented in the ensuing chapter.

BEST PRACTICE

The foundation of this section was edited and modified from information provided in Cova and Cova's 2004 paper, "Tribal marketing: the tribalization of society and its impact on the conduct of marketing." The paper can also be found in the January 2002 special issue of *European Journal of Marketing* (p. 595).

When Salomon made a decision to enter the burgeoning snowboard market, they knew that their marketing approach would need to be different. Snowboarders were not like other sport and ski consumers. They were, in fact, a tribe. Salomon decided to keep a low profile in order to "listen" in the market. They embarked on a program of observing participants and learning about the market. Their next move was to involve tribe members as a marketing unit in the development of specific logos (apart from existing Salomon products) and product design. Launching the products would not be accomplished through traditional channels. At the winter sports trade shows, Salomon products were displayed at Pro-Shop booths, not the mega booth that Salomon occupied. They opted for no advertising but rather a presence at summer snowboard camps and the support (dare you say sponsorship) of a team of expert boarders. They went to the slopes and offered test rides with little emphasis on selling. This "in-the-market marketing" was very effective and positioned Salomon as an "authentic" supporter of the tribe. The results of their activities allowed Salomon to move from no products to the #3 position in the market within two years.

NIKE GLOBAL BRAND PLAN 2004–2006

Guiding Principles

To bring inspiration and innovation to every athlete in the world

If you have a body, you are an athlete

Underlying Beliefs

Maxim 1: It is our nature to innovate

Maxim 2: Nike is a company

Maxim 3: Nike is a brand

Maxim 4: Simplify and go

Maxim 5: The consumer decides

Maxim 6: Be a sponge

Maxim 7: Evolve immediately

Maxim 8: Do the right thing

Maxim 9: Master the fundamentals

Maxim 10: We are on the offense—always.

Fundamental values that guide the brand

INSPIRE
- Promote a sense of possibility for every athlete
- Celebrate the power of sport and the joy of movement

INNOVATE
- Make possible new levels of performance
- Do the unexpected
- Take consumers someplace new

FOCUS
- Saturate every product and communication with the distinctive Nike point of view
- Presume nothing
- Listen to everything

CONNECT
- Create a dialogue with consumers
- Build long-term relationships with core athletic consumers

CARE
- Live up to our responsibility as global citizens

Brand Development Principle

Strategically expand the brand and "own the edge" in consumers' minds.

Strategic Framework

Build the brand through athletes, participants, and influencers.

- *Athletes*
  "Nike inspires me through sports . . . they understand my performance needs."

- *Participants*
  "Nike inspires me to participate . . . they understand my functional needs."

- *Influencers*
  "Nike inspires me through culture and product . . . they fit my personality."

Brand Drivers

Authentic Sport

- Performance needs of athletes
- Inside the sport

Active Life

- Performance needs of active consumers

Connected

- Brand for me
- They understand my world

Consumer Platforms—Position the brand and drive the business globally

- Basketball—The art and expression of "the players' game"
- Football—"Brilliant Football"
- Apparel—"Designed for movement"
- Women's training—"Passion in action"
- Running—"Personal best"

Marketing Strategy Worksheets

The worksheets provide a guide for developing various sections of a marketing plan. The following sheets cover marketing strategies, including market penetration, market share development, product development, diversification, and their impact on resources. Complete these worksheets as a preparatory step in the creation of a marketing plan

Select and articulate all appropriate market strategies that you intend to include in your marketing plan.

Market Penetration.

_____
_____
_____
_____
_____
_____
_____
_____
_____
_____

Market Share Development.

_____
_____
_____
_____
_____
_____

_____
_____
_____
_____
_____

Product Development.

_____
_____
_____
_____
_____
_____
_____
_____
_____
_____

Diversification.

_____
_____
_____
_____
_____
_____
_____
_____
_____
_____

Discuss the impact that each strategy will have on organizational resources.

_____
_____
_____
_____
_____
_____
_____
_____
_____
_____

Chapter Seven

MARKETING MIX

Marketing Mix

The tools for implementing strategy include the 4 Ps of marketing, mentioned earlier in the workbook (product, price, place, and promotion) (McCarthy & Perreault, 1990). The interplay between each of these four variables constitutes the marketing mix. Research in 2004 (Nielsen, 2004) found that the interaction or "mix" of these marketing elements effected sport consumers. When asked which factors most influenced their decision of where to shop for sporting goods, 91% of consumers said, "the store carries the product I need." Eighty-one percent said it was the price of the item, while 63% attributed the store's image and reputation followed by "a special promotional event or sale" (58%). Each has a significant interaction effect on the others. For example, Ely Callaway, founder of Callaway Golf, commented "we wouldn't have the biggest selling golf clubs in the world and at the highest prices [about $1600 per set of irons] if we didn't have a good product" (Torsiello, 1998, p. 16). There is a strong connection between price and quality. Ask somebody if given a choice of a ticket to a basketball game for free if they want a $50 ticket or a $75 ticket. The answer will probably be $75, even though they had no knowledge of the location of the ticket. Furthermore, Pallerino noted, "when you slash your prices down to the 'next to nothing' level, the consumer starts to question the quality of your product" (Pallerino, 2004, p. 4). Pitts and Stotlar (2007) provide an in-depth analysis about the marketing mix in *Fundamentals of Sport Marketing*. However, an overview of the concept is presented on the subsequent pages.

PRODUCT

In sport, an exact characterization of products is exceedingly difficult. Pitts and Stotlar (2007) refer to a product mix as the set of all product lines and items that a particular organization makes available to consumers. For example, adidas markets shoes for 43 different sports including jogging, racing, cycling, weight lifting, and windsurfing. Furthermore, adidas shoes were available in 260 specific models and 640 various styles, and the company reached $8.3 billion in sales. Even the standards for production of basketballs have undergone change. In 2003, both the National Federation of State High School Associations and the NCAA modified rules to allow the use of synthetic basketballs. In addition, new technology was producing balls with 10 panels instead of the traditional 8, in order to improve the handling characteristics of the ball.

In the sporting goods manufacturing business, competition is fierce. For example, Reebok's product strategy in the athletic shoe market is to have a new model arriving in the marketplace every 45 days. The life cycle of any one model can range anywhere from three to six months, when graphics and colors may change dramatically, or an entirely new model may be introduced. Changes in market share and profitability result in multimillion-dollar gains and losses.

Some sports organizations only sell services. Many professional sports agents sell their services to professional athletes for contract negotiations, endorsements, and financial management. Massage therapists also provide services in the sport industry. Other consultants provide services ranging from coaching to sport facility design. The service sector of the sport industry truly is immense.

As previously shown, producing, marketing, and selling products is a serious endeavor. Sport marketing's goal is to meet the needs of consumers, not to focus on particular products an organization produces. The Hillerich and Bradsby Company (e.g., Louisville Slugger) went through considerable change on the road to dominance in the baseball bat industry. The original philosophy of the company was one of product orientation— "sell what you make." In the specialized industry of making custom bats for major league players, there was limited profitability. A change in the company's outlook, provided by Bradsby joining the firm, resulted in a market orientation to "make what will sell." The realization of this concept for the company was to shift to mass production of baseball bats from custom "hand tooled" production. Refinement was necessary as well because the market for full sized major league bats was not nearly as great (or profitable) as that of children's bats modeled after major league bats (Pitts and Fielding, 1989). The end result was that the corporation began to see consumers in a much broader view, eventually coming full circle to meet the demands of a large market segment with significant demands for the product.

Extending this concept of meeting customer needs, one company in Colorado was able to increase its sales by 400% in one year by moving from mass marketing to a smaller market niche. In the growing segment of outdoor equipment, many manufacturers had designed backpacks based on the male torso. However, many women found these backpacks uncomfortable. To meet this need, Grand West Outfitters designed and marketed backpacks designed specifically for women. Demand for the products was so high that the company had difficulty keeping those backpacks in stock. Thus, comparing the two scenarios, you can't always decide that specialized products are "bad" and that mass marketed products are "good."

Golf is a sport continually inundated with new products. The late 1980s saw major controversies arise in the design of the grooves on the face of the golf club. A square groove was supposed to reduce the in-flight effects on the ball due to errors in hitting. Certain clubs were banned, causing a tremendous amount of publicity and increased sales. Similar controversy over golf ball design has been rampant in the industry. Each innovation in product design made consumers more aware of their need for improved products and moved them closer to purchase.

Several innovations occurred in golf club design and construction material during the 1990s. The introduction of oversized club faces, graphite shafts, and new alloy metals contributed to the advances in club construction. As a result, the sales of golf equipment exploded during the decade.

After purchasing new clubs, many golfers were amazed at the improvements in their game. Many noted hitting the ball significantly farther than with their previous set. However, the performance increases that the golfers were experiencing may not have been due to the new materials and design of the clubs. An interesting study was conducted in 1997, examining the features of many of these new clubs. For many years, golf clubs had "generally accepted standards in both length of the club and the degree of face loft assigned to each [club] number in the set. A 5-iron, for instance, is normally made with a loft of 30 degrees and is usually 37 inches long" (Pollard, 1997, p. 47). For the average consumer, it would be very difficult to ascertain the degree of loft for a club face. "So what manufacturers are doing these days is shipping out sets of clubs with stronger lofts and extra length. Hesto presto, you can hit longer" (Pollard, 1997, p. 47). Pollard revealed that the average 5-iron he studied had a 27.04-degree of loft and was 37.75 inches long. Similarly, the Senior King Cobra pitching wedge which should have had a 50-degree loft had a 43-degree loft and a 36.5 inch shaft, almost identical to an 8-iron. To hit farther, Pollard recommends that customers save their money and simply select a lower numbered club.

Sports marketers should, through their marketing information systems, attempt to determine the answers to these questions as part of benefit segmentation in market analysis. This reintroduces the concepts of core product and product extension (presented in Chapter 2). The core product relates to the central item that is being marketed: the game, the team, the shoes, or the equipment. A product extension is a product or service that is sold or marketed to enhance the core product. In the early 1900s, Hillerich and Bradsby offered a hitting guidebook with every Louisville Slugger sold. Similarly, Spalding included instructions on pitching technique with their baseballs. These items were not the central product—the bat and the ball were. Yet, a component product which customers valued was also offered (Pitts & Fielding, 1989).

Similar to the development of new products, innovation also exists in the service industry. Jake Steinfeld, fitness professional, pioneered a new service called one-to-one training in the 1980s. His service, "Body by Jake," involved traveling to the client's home for the delivery of fitness consultations and training. This concept was not entirely different from private lessons in tennis, golf, or many other sports, but it had never before been applied to the fitness field. The success of the idea was that almost all clubs and professionals now offer personal training services as a part of the fitness business.

Regardless of whether an organization is marketing a physical product, an athletic event, or a service, you must construct a thorough product definition and analysis as a part of their marketing efforts. Only when an organization has a true understanding of what it is that they are offering can they proceed with the other elements of sport marketing.

PRICE

Probably the most often manipulated and least understood of the marketing elements is price. Price is the amount of money (or item of equivalent value) asked or paid for your products or services in the exchange process. Economists will argue this is the key element that will determine success or failure. Marketers, on the other hand, will contend that it is but one of the essential elements. Part of their rationale is that, regardless of the price, a poor product will not sell. Arguments have also been made concerning whether pricing is a science or an art. The science advocates forward successive formulas for determining the best possible price, while the art theorists suggest that other sociological factors are extremely important in pricing decisions.

Several pricing theories are available for examination: price elasticity, supply-demand, utility, marginal costing, etc. No exhaustive review of these theories will be attempted; rather, a broad overall view of pricing will be offered, allowing the reader to construct a basic framework for decision making. A significantly more detailed discussion of pricing theory is depicted in *Fundamentals of Sport Marketing* (Pitts & Stotlar, 2007).

Generally stated, price elasticity of demand relates to how demand changes in relationship to changes in price. According to Kotler and Armstrong (2006, p. 318), "if demand hardly changes with a small increase in price, we say the demand is inelastic. If demand changes greatly, we say the demand is elastic." The ratio of change is critical such that in some situations more profits can result, even if fewer units are sold.

Miller, Shaad, Burch, and Turner (1999) discussed various issues related to supply and demand pricing. In many stadiums and arenas, the locations available for signage are almost endless. However, most sponsors would prefer locations near the court/field and in the field of TV coverage rather than a location on the mezzanine. Therefore, if the demand is greater for prime locations, the price can be adjusted upward. Specifically, the authors cited an example from an indoor professional soccer team. The public relations director was reviewing revenues with one of the managing partners, recalling their ability to sell the entire dasher board inventory for another consecutive year. Based on a supply-demand basis, the managing partner suggested that the price for the dasher boards should be raised $150 per year (10%) until the demand decreased. The net result of the implementation of this strategy was that within 10 years, the price of the dasher boards had doubled.

A general starting point is to examine the relationship between volume and profit. It is obvious, even to the novice sport marketer, that there is a direct relationship between the two variables. You can make a million dollars either by making $1.00 profit on each item, selling 1 million units, or you can just sell one unit with a million dollar profit margin (the trick is to sell that one).

Many sport companies use a traditional cost-oriented pricing structure that begins with a calculation of the cost of production, marketing, and distribution. To this figure, the manufacturer adds its desired profit margin (Stevens, Loudon, Wrenn, & Warren, 1997). Eventually, wholesalers and retailers add desired profit margins to arrive at the final retail price. Sporting goods stores, souvenir shops, and other retailers often employ this pricing technique. One term that you should be familiar with is "Keystone." This commonly means that the wholesale cost of the item is doubled in order to achieve a reasonable profit margin. The main shortcoming of this pricing method is that total profits cannot be estimated without knowing the sales volume. All that can be calculated is the profit per unit. To overcome this deficiency, some companies employ a breakeven pricing method.

Breakeven Analysis

Sports marketers often use a breakeven analysis as a starting point for product pricing. The purpose of the analysis is to determine how many units must be sold at a given price to fully cover costs. The costs are calculated from two important factors: fixed costs (those which do not vary with output volume) that relate to items such as salary, machinery, or facility rental and variable costs (those which do vary with output volume) that relate to the cost of materials and shipping. These should be figured on a per unit basis to minimize price calculation. The result is a total cost, which is achieved by adding the fixed costs and variable costs factors together (Cohen, 1998; Mullin, Hardy, and Sutton, 2007).

Total Cost = Fixed Costs + (Variable Costs [per unit] × Volume)

To illustrate the principle, two simplified examples, one with a physical product and one relating to a service, are provided (see Figure 7.1; Figure 7.2).

Scenario: You find the backpacks you have been using do not meet the needs of many customers because they currently come in only two sizes, too big and too small. You decide that if you can create a backpack that will fold up and convert from big to small, based on the needs of the user at various times, you could make your fortune. In designing and producing the product, you find that your costs include the following:

FIXED COSTS
Equipment purchase. $100,000.00
Salary and Benefits (one employee) $55,000.00
Facility Lease $12,000.00
Utilities $6,000.00
Start-up Capital. $15,000.00
Advertising/Marketing $5,000.00

Total $193,000.00

VARIABLE COSTS (at a production volume of 10,000)
Materials (cloth, zippers, buckles, etc.) $10,000.00
Shipping $1,000.00

Total $11,000.00

Total Cost= $204,000 to produce 10,000 backpacks   *(continued on next page)*

Figure 7.1. Acme Backpack Company Breakeven Analysis

(continued from previous page)

The breakeven calculation is figured by dividing the total cost by the number of backpacks produced.

$$\text{Breakeven} = \frac{\textit{Total cost}}{\text{Number produced}} = \text{Price}$$

or

$$\text{Breakeven} = \frac{\$204,000.00}{10,000} = \$20.40$$

Therefore, each of the backpacks would have to be sold for $20.40 to break even. Unfortunately, a wholesale cost of $20.40 appears to be too high to allow for wholesalers and retailers to make a profit. To remedy the situation, you may look at producing more units in order to lower the cost of each unit.

If the production volume was planned as 50,000 units, the analysis would look like this:

FIXED COSTS

Equipment purchase:	$100,000.00
Salary and Benefits (one employee)	$55,000.00
Facility Lease	$12,000.00
Utilities	$6,000.00
Start-up Capital	$15,000.00
Advertising/Marketing	$5,000.00
Total	$193,000.00

VARIABLE COSTS (at a production volume of 50,000)

Materials (cloth, zippers, buckles, etc.)	$50,000.00
Shipping	$5,000.00
Total	$55,000.00

Total Cost= $248,000 to produce 50,000 backpacks

The breakeven calculation is figured by dividing the total cost by the number of backpacks produced.

$$\text{Breakeven} = \frac{\$248,000.00}{50,000} = \$4.26$$

In this case, each of the backpacks would have to be sold for only $4.26 to break even.

The mathematical manipulation of this formula is also of value to the sport marketer. If you decided that you could charge wholesalers $10.00 for the product, how many would you have to sell to breakeven if you still manufactured the 50,000?

$$\text{Breakeven} = \frac{\$248,000.00}{24,800} = \$10.00$$

In this situation, the first 24,800 are contributing to the reduction of fixed costs, but the remaining units are adding to profits.

Figure 7.1. Acme Backpack Company Breakeven Analysis (continued)

The advantages of the breakeven pricing method are that it is relatively simple to calculate from an administrative perspective and that it is fair to both buyers and sellers because it does not inflate prices during periods of high demand, yet it still allows producers a reasonable profit (Kotler & Armstrong, 2006). Reese and Mittlestadt (2001) listed "revenue needs of the organization" as one of the top factors

Scenario: As the coach of the University's basketball program, you desire to run a five-day, summer basketball day camp for youth. The breakeven analysis could look something like this:

FIXED COSTS
Equipment purchase:...$500.00
Salary and Benefits (three coaches) $15,000.00
Facility Lease...$500.00
Advertising and mailing *$2,000.00*

Total	$18,000.00

Variable Costs (at a camp volume of 100)
T-shirts...$500.00
Lunch $2,500.00

Total	$3,000.00

Total Cost= $21,000 to hold a basketball camp for 100 participants

The breakeven calculation is figured by dividing the total cost by the number of players in the camp.

$$\text{Breakeven} = \frac{\$21,000.00}{100} = \$210.00$$

Therefore, each of the players would have to be charged $210.00 to break even.

If the desired volume is planned as 150 campers, the analysis would look like this:

FIXED COSTS
Equipment purchase:...$500.00
Salary and Benefits (three coaches) $15,000.00
Facility Lease...$500.00
Advertising and mailing $2,000.00

Total	$18,000.00

VARIABLE COSTS (at a camp volume of 150)
T-shirts...$750.00
Lunch $3,750.00

Total	$4,500.00

Total Cost= $22,500 to hold a basketball camp for 150 participants

$$\text{Breakeven} = \frac{\$22,500.00}{150} = \$150.00$$

In this case, each of the players would have to be charged only $150.00 to breakeven. Some arguments could be made that the coaching cost is not fixed but, instead, a variable cost. When you keep adding players, at some point you must increase the number of coaches. The same argument could be made for leasing factory warehouses such that at some volume additional staff/square-footage must be secured.

Figure 7.2. Anywhere University Basketball Camp Breakeven Analysis

in NFL teams' pricing philosophy. Cohen (1998) recognized problems with this method because it does not take into account a variety of market conditions, such as demand and competition. With today's sophisticated level of market analysis, shorter product life cycles, economic volatility, and increased customer knowledge, use of this method alone may be outdated. It is, however, an important tool in developing a pricing strategy.

Demand-Oriented Pricing

Additional pricing concepts include demand orientation, competition orientation, and product quality orientation (Stevens et al., 1997). Demand orientation is directly focused on the strength of the market you wish to serve. This is particularly useful in sport marketing. Any attempt to use cost-oriented pricing for athletic events is incredibly difficult, if not impossible, to achieve. But, you can estimate how much consumers are willing to spend on a ticket. Therefore, the demand-oriented method of pricing is more subjective than objective.

Many of professional sports teams have entered into variable ticket pricing. The Colorado Rockies (MLB) franchise was among the first to vary the price of their tickets based on the opponent. It was based on the question, "Are our 81 home games identical products?" Team executives decided the answer was no. Teams where there was a high rivalry with the Rockies were priced higher. These were designated as "Premium Games." They also differentiated the pricing structure through "Value" games and "Marquee" games. Based on the success (or lack of revolt), many other teams implemented similar pricing structures. Even at the collegiate level, there are some who advocate variable pricing. Steinbach (2002) noted that teams like Michigan and Ohio State could double the price of their annual duel in football. The University of California set its standard football ticket prices at $27 but increased the price to $35 for games against USC and UCLA, and set the price for the match-up with Stanford at $50. One sport economist commented, "We see a lot of ticket scalping at certain games. Fans are essentially paying that price anyway, it might as well go to the athletic department" (Steinbach, 2002, p. 24.)

In an attempt to decrease subjectivity, many marketers engage in market research specific to price. In an effort to determine the price points for tickets to the 2002 Winter Olympic Games, the organizing committee sold sets of ticket on eBay and let the demand for the tickets drive the price. They eventually backed off of those prices a bit, but the high demand tickets for ice-skating and opening ceremonies were priced higher than those for cross-country skiing.

This has also been called "demand-backward" pricing. Through this technique, marketers start with the price that research has suggested consumers are willing to pay and then adjust product quality, marketing costs, and profit margins to arrive at the market price. The strategy can be particularly successful if you have identified an opportunity in the market at a particular price-point.

Other demand-oriented factors are based on place or time. Many sports organizations offer different prices for tickets based on seat location. Front row seats are more expensive than those in the upper deck. With regard to time, golf courses charge more in green fees for play on the weekend than they charge for play during the week. This "prime" vs. "nonprime" timing can also be seen in the ski industry where early and late season ski passes are cheaper than those during the winter holidays. Each of these pricing policies is based upon the demand that consumers have shown for the particular products. Other variations in pricing are high season rates, play-off tickets, and age rates (children, senior citizen).

An organization must also be extremely careful in examining only total revenues. In some cases, an organization is interested in the percentage of total revenue that is profit. If a basketball costs $5.00 to produce and the manufacturing company desires a $5.00 profit on each unit sold at wholesale, they charge retailers $10.00 for each ball ordered. The retailer might sell the ball for anywhere between $20–30 (for example, the Wilson NCAA composite, indoor/outdoor basketball lists for $24.99). If the price to the retailer is reduced by $2.50, the manufacturing company is giving them a 25% reduction. The truth of the matter is that the manufacturing company just reduced profits by 50% (from $5.00 gross margin to $2.50 gross margin). Although the company would only have to sell 1.33 times as many balls to equal the same total revenues, they will have to sell 2 times as many to receive the same amount of profit. Similar pricing decisions could surround Spalding's Official NBA leather basketball that retails for about $100. Their profit margin may be smaller, but because of the price, total revenues accrued as profit might be higher.

In calculating profit as a percentage of gain, examine the following situation where a company was considering an expansion with current profits at $10 million on gross sales of $100 million. Profit returned is 10%. Under the expansion, if the company increases its gross sales volume to $150 million but their percentage of return was to drop to 7%, would a smart company still consider the expansion? The calculations show that, even though the ratio of return decreased, the company still increased profits by $500,000.

In sport, variable pricing is often reflected in discounting. Discounting can occur when customers buy in large quantities, pay cash, or are members of a particular group (institutional alumni, co-op buying program, senior citizen, children, etc.). Other discount variables in sport include high/low season and peak/off periods. The high/low season is used by many resorts in the pricing of their packages and the peak/off periods are used by fitness centers and golf courses, both differentiate pricing in times of low demand. Many sporting goods companies will offer reduced prices on team uniforms if they are ordered in advance of the season, times when the production facilities are not running at full capacity.

Spoelstra (1997) recommends that an organization refrain from too much discounting of ticket prices to sports events. In his experience with professional sport, discounting lowered the value in the mind of the consumer. In one promotion with the New Jersey Nets, a campaign to heavily discount a five game package was not successful in attracting new fans. However, an alternative strategy of adding value to the purchase resulted in the sale of an additional 12,000 tickets. Rather than discounting the ticket price by a set percentage, use that same percentage of money to add promotional products to the package. In the instance cited, Spoelstra added a free basketball, team logo hat, and a team poster for fans who purchased the package. This was accomplished for less money than the cost of discounting and generated $1.5 million in new sales.

Promotional pricing is characterized by the reduction of the product price for a specific time. Although it is often thought of as an introduction strategy, it can also be effective when utilized during the product life cycle. The sport marketer must be cautious in promotional pricing to prevent consumers from establishing the promotional price in their mind. This would make it difficult to reinstate the normal suggested retail price. Most consumers are sophisticated enough to realize that, if profits are generated at a promotional price, then the normal retail price will result in exorbitant profits. Needless to say, this does not create positive consumer-company relationships.

Moving the consumer toward more expensive purchases is also a common marketing strategy. As discussed in previous chapters of the text, most sports marketers work with a product line, which is a spread of products with varying features and benefits. As previously mentioned, ski bindings were offered with a variety of benefits in a price spread from which the consumer could choose. The task was to determine the features and the price that best met the needs (or perceived needs) of the consumer. Several sports organizations spend a great deal of their marketing efforts attempting to move the consumer to higher-priced purchases. For instance, many golf shops begin sales discussions with moderately priced clubs. However, they quickly begin to show customers more expensive sets with graphite shafts and special alloy club heads. The intent is to move the consumer to a more expensive product. If you have an event rather than a physical product, a ticket price spread can accomplish this feat.

Almost all stadiums and areas have a spread in ticket prices. This strategy allows consumers to make independent pricing decisions. Based upon the benefit received, each consumer evaluates the options and completes the transaction. Without a price spread, they may not purchase at all. In addition, many buyers automatically buy in the middle of the price range, based on a perception of improved benefit; yet in reality, there may be less expensive seats that provide as good a view. Coors Field, home of the Colorado Rockies baseball team, sells selected tickets (called the Rock Pile) for $5.00 ($1.00 for children). These seats are almost as good as some seats costing twice as much. In this, as in other stadiums (i.e., Wrigley Field in Chicago), there is also a collective attractiveness that has attached itself to the "cheap seats."

Even in the area of concessions, a marketer can move people up to higher-priced items through semantics. A recent trend in the labeling of soft drinks sizes has been very successful in this endeavor. Traditional terminology in the business labeled sizes as small, medium, and large, although some concessionaires have moved to a slate of offerings that include mini (or child's) in place of small, then medium, and large. This typically moves the consumer up one position when he/she would have previously ordered a small.

Earlier in the text (Chapter 3), examples were given of the processes available for analyzing the competition. All pricing strategies should be attentive to market movement and the actions of competitors. Over time an organization can gain a clear indication of industry trends and market extremes so that they can price products favorably when compared to the competition.

Another general category of pricing strategy is skimming, which most often involves innovative and high priced items (Pride & Ferrell, 2008). Here, the price is set at the highest value that the company believes the customer will pay. Being the first in the marketplace with a highly anticipated product or service can give a corner on the market and allow a higher price to be charged. As others enter the market, the resources received in the skimming stage are used to fight the competition on other fronts, such as advertising or distribution channels. Another tactic is to attempt to keep the selling price stable as the competitors enter the market but reduce the wholesale cost to retailers, which enhances their profit margin on the product when compared to the competition's.

PLACE (DISTRIBUTION)

The place of distribution cannot be changed as easily as the price or the product/service. Place can range from the retail site of a sporting goods outlet, to a stadium or arena where events take place, and to a client's home where the delivery of personal fitness training occurs. Its function as a marketing element is to link the consumer with the sport product or service. For more information, *Fundamentals of Sport Marketing* (Pitts & Stotlar, 2007) presents considerable information on this marketing mix element.

In retail sporting goods, as with most retail operations, the three most important business decisions made are location, location, and location. Several steps are essential in arriving at a sound decision. As with the entire marketing process, begin with an analysis of customers, competition, and market. This market analysis is accomplished by plotting the proposed store site on a map and examining the customer base available (through census data or market research publications), the access to the location from major highways, and supply/demand factors within the industry.

Location is an extremely important factor in the placement of fitness centers. In one study, research found that 84% of club members rated location as the single most important reason for joining the club. In addition, they noted the maximum drive time clients would tolerate was 15–20 minutes if the facility had a pool, or 10 minutes if it did not. "The message is simple, don't waste your marketing budget on trying to attract an audience from outside your primary market" (Browes, 1998, p. 41)

The location of a sports operation has a considerable impact on corporate image. With this in mind, some companies are very particular about where their products are sold. You cannot go into a discount store and find the high end of a shoe company's line. These are simply not items that the store feels that it can sell. At times, though, the manufacturer makes the decision. Some of them may only allow discount chains to sell low-end products. In 2003, the sport nutrition company Experimental and Applied Sciences (EAS) made the decision to allow its supplements to be sold through Wal-Mart and assorted grocery stores, as opposed selling exclusively through its corporately owned channels. Many believed that these actions damaged the well-earned image of EAS as an upscale product, but total sales and profits increased substantially at a time when the company was looking to go public. Both Nike and Callaway made decisions in 2004 to make their golf balls available through Target stores. While this may negatively affect their image, Target will move a lot of product, and both companies reserve their highest quality balls for sale in pro shops. Some sporting goods suppliers intentionally restrict retailers of their products to retain a prestigious image. Golf ball manufacturer Slazenger sells its balls only through pro shops. While the price of ordinary golf balls may be as low as $18.00 per dozen at a discount store, Slazenger balls sell for more than $50 per dozen at the pro shops. However, there seems to be sufficient capacity in the $1.2 billion golf ball market for both high-end and entry-level products.

Ticket distribution in sport is an area that has undergone dynamic change. In years past, fans had to line up at the ticket window in order to purchase a ticket to an event. With the proliferation of web credit cards, ordering tickets was a mere phone call to the box office away. Then, the industry changed again with purchase availability from off-site companies like Stubhub and Ticketmaster. According to Miller and Fielding (1997), "Ticketron became the first company to offer computerized ticket distribution in 1968. In 1991 Ticketmaster acquired Ticketron" (p. 48). Their research indicated that 76% of the professional sport teams utilized the services of computerized ticketing companies, with Ticketmaster garnering the major share (66%).

Ticketmaster appears to be the major force in the industry but competes with as many as 16 other firms in professional sport. Tickets.com has also established itself as a principal agent in on-line ticket sales (Miller & Fielding, 1997). These innovative companies make tickets to a variety of events even more accessible to consumers. Online ticketing has seen phenomenal growth through Internet access. Projections for online ticket sales were estimated at $1.2 billion for 2007 (Greenspan, 2003). The accumulated effect of this technology has been greater attendance and happier sports fans (Miller & Fielding, 1997).

Virtual Place

Sometimes "place" is not a place. In 2007, more than 1.5 billion people were connected to the worldwide web, and approximately half of US internet users regularly purchase items directly online. While the scope of this book precludes a full discussion of electronic commerce (or the e-corporation), it is important to explore the possibilities presented in retailing over the Internet. Kotler and Armstrong (2006, p. 555) define e-commerce as "buying and selling processes supported by electronic means, primarily the Internet. E-commerce includes e-marketing and e-purchasing." Brown (2003, p. 49) said, "sport marketers must understand how this technology works as an effective marketing tool." While 13% of all Internet users are shopping (Zhang & Won, 2004), it is estimated that only 2% of all retail transactions were conducted over the Internet. However, 2% of all sales in some industries represent substantial market share and income potential (Kim, 2004). As a result of this surge in Internet use, $6.64 billion was spent on Internet advertising in 2003, with $230 million spent on sport-related web sites (Internet Advertising Bureau, 2003; King, 2003). Overall, 70% of internet-based sports retailers reported positive operating margins. Therefore, your "place" may actually be a "cyber-place." Virtual retailing is attributed to lower marketing, fulfillment, and customer service costs. The end results were the ability to lower the cost of goods sold (Miller & Veltri, 2004).

With the increased availability of broadband (high speed) technology, the sport industry increasingly offers fans subscription services for teams and online data, as well as fantasy leagues. Total revenues for 2008 from broadband subscriptions in the sport industry were projected to top $6.4 billion (Greenspan, 2003). Only a few years ago, no one would have predicted that consumers would be able to access event tickets, watch sports broadcasts, and purchase products from web sites via their cell phones.

As previously noted, today's consumers want customized products, which provide solutions that match their needs, not mass-marketed products in the "one size fits all" tradition (Kotler & Armstrong, 2006). Fullerton (2007, p. 208) referred to this scenario as "the vanishing mass market." Consumers increasingly want products on their terms, at their time, and in a convenient manner. Where shopping malls provided convenience over the last few decades, the Internet provides increased convenience today. Does the phrase location, location, location apply to the Internet? Yes; with a web site, companies can be everywhere for everyone, open 24 hours a days, seven days per week (Hamel, 1998).

The impact that e-commerce retailing has on the marketing mix is immense. Customers are able to price shop in a matter of seconds. Internet shopping is very much about price, because customers can move from one location on the web to another quite rapidly. Subsequently, marketers of sport products and services must be competitive with other companies on price.

The Internet is more than just an electronic catalog. Through a web site, a company can communicate better with customers than it can through a catalog because a web site offers an interactive interface between customers and the company. For instance, if a customer is shopping for running shoes, the web site can be configured to present a series of questions about the training patterns of the customer and lead the customer to a variety of products that fit the training regiment of the client. The site can also prompt the customer for other items that may be of interest by asking related questions such as, "Need some running shorts?"

Miller and Veltri (2004) noted that consumers are motivated to purchase online by improved service, better value, greater selection, and ease of purchasing. Across sport product categories (shoes, apparel, equipment, video games, and memorabilia), the consumers consistently ranked selection as a top factor in their decision.

However, there are a few drawbacks to e-commerce. One limitation is that customers can't try on the shoes. Another is that delivery of the product is not immediate. Overnight delivery is available but often at an additional cost that does not exist in retail outlets. Furthermore, some consumers still harbor concerns over the security of online purchases.

Hamel (1998, p. 88) suggests, "individual consumers will be issuing RFPs [requests for proposals] just like the largest industrial buyers. Make no mistake, the Web will drive the last nail into the coffin of set prices." He proposes that consumers will put their purchase demands out for bid. Who will provide the best price for the newest set of Callaway golf clubs?

The web also presents enormous possibilities for distribution of sports events. Major League Baseball put together a deal with AOL for the 2005 and 2006 season that would provide live game audio and video highlights to AOL subscribers. The deal generated $50 million for MLB in cash and services (Adams, 2004).

PROMOTION

Promotion has been described and a catch-all category for a number of marketing activities (Mullin, Hardy, & Sutton, 2007). It has been called the marketing communication mix (Kotler & Armstrong, 2006). Typically, this communications and promotions mix includes advertising, sales promotions, public relations, personal selling, and direct marketing. Stevens, Loudon, Wrenn, and Warren (1997, p. 224) commented that promotions "are the most visible manifestation" of your marketing efforts. So much so that many people in the general public (and unfortunately, some inside the corporation) believe that promotions are synonymous with marketing. However, most marketing managers understand that promotions are merely a part of the overall marketing plan and are an ingredient in the marketing mix. That said, promotion and the communications mix are recognized as powerful components in the overall marketing mix and given considerable attention in Pitts and Stotlar's *Fundamentals of Sport Marketing* (2007).

Pride and Ferrell (2008) noted that promotional activities can create awareness, stimulate demand, increase the likelihood of product trial, and retain loyal customers. Mullin et al. (2007) used the AIDA acronym to denote the purposes of promotions in Increasing *A*wareness, Attracting *I*nterest, Arousing *D*esire, and Initiating *A*ction. A successful sales promotion undertaken by the California Angels (MLB—now the Los Angeles Angels of Anaheim) was to celebrate the grand opening (and sell season tickets) of the renovated Edison Field through a "sneak preview" arranged for potential customers. By calling a toll free number, prospects could attend an advance tour of the stadium, meet players, and sit in seats that could be purchased for the upcoming season. This activity was very successful and contributed to a substantial increase in season ticket sales.

Promotional activities have proven to be successful in professional sport settings. The popular "hat day" and "bat day" product giveaways have had varying degrees of success (Mullin et al., 2007). Major League Baseball's 2003 research showed that although bat day only produced an attendance increase of 14%, small replicas of the ball park was the best promotional giveaway—generating an increase of 58%. Beach towels increased the turnstile count 31% overall but generated an increase of 86% for weekday games (Most effective, 2003). Boyd and Kregbiel (2003) found that promotions were responsible for a 19.6% increase in attendance in their study of MLB. An example of one promotion by the Colorado Rockies is presented in the Best Practice section of this chapter. Overall, in-arena promotions have been found to be effective in increasing attendance.

The family name most associated with outrageous sports promotions is Veeck. The late Bill Veeck, former owner and operator of the Chicago White Sox and Cleveland Indians, is credited with introducing electronic scoreboards and names on player jerseys. However, he is most noted for sending a midget (little person) to bat for the MLB St. Louis Browns in 1951. Although it garnered more attention than he had anticipated, it also drew the fury of the league office. Following in his father's footsteps, minor league owner and consultant to a number of professional teams, Mike Veeck has also developed his share of effective promotions. Among the most popular was his Mime-O-Vision, where Veeck hired mimes to reenact plays during the game in place of the traditional instant replays. Fans were so upset by the actions that they began pelting the mimes with hotdogs, replete with mustard and ketchup. The frenzy was on. The concession stand soon sold out of hotdogs, but everyone (excluding the mime) had a great time. In other promotions, Veeck created "Call in Sick Day," where the team would fax excuses into a fan's worksite so they could attend the game, and "Vasectomy Night," slated for Father's day, which would give some lucky fan a free vasectomy. His "Nobody Night" with the minor league Charleston Riverdogs went into the record books for the lowest attended game. Veeck locked the fans out of the stadium until the sixth inning (after official attendance was recorded) entertaining them in the stadium parking lot with food and big screen images of the game inside. Regarding his philosophy on promotions, Veeck commented that you should "make 75 percent of the crowd laugh, annoy 15 percent, and who cares about the other 10 percent" (Lidz, Kenndey, & Deitch, 2002, p. 25). The 2007 "Michael Vick Chew Toy" giveaway was one of his more recent ventures.

Within the marketing mix, promotions can be further divided into the elements of relations, advertising, publicity, and personal selling (Cohen, 1998; Pride & Ferrell, 2008). The scope of this workbook does not provide for a detailed discussion of these elements. Therefore, refer to *Fundamentals of Sport Marketing* (Pitts & Stotlar, 2007).

BEST PRACTICE

Colorado Rockies Baseball Club

Program Title: Ladies Night and Ladies Fan Club

Objective: The Colorado Rockies' main objective with this promotion was to increase female fan attendance on a regular basis.

Program Description: Mothers, daughters, sisters, and neighbors will all come out to Coors Field because the Colorado Rockies are continuing their successful "Ladies Night" promotion this season! Last season, this initiative was such a hit that the Rockies brought it back for a second run—every Wednesday home game at Coors Field is "Ladies Night!" Here's how the program works:

First, every female—of any age—that comes through the gates on these special Wednesday home games gets a voucher for a free ticket to a future game of her choice. These vouchers are one of the most highly redeemed vouchers of any program the Rockies run.

Second, and the best deal of all, the Ladies Fan Club Package gives women the opportunity to attend each and every "Ladies Night" for an exceptionally low price of $99. This package included two tickets in the special Ladies Fan Club sections for each of the twelve Wednesday "Ladies Night" games throughout the season. Also included in the package were a commemorative jersey and the promise of exclusive festivities and opportunities throughout the season.

The special festivities and opportunities in the membership include: Scorekeeping Clinic, Baseball Clinic, Autograph Session, Baseball Bingo, All-Star Ballot, and/or Trivia Contests. Also, this season the Rockies will hold a "talk show" led by one of the Rockies' wives with special interviews and opportunities for Q&A.

Media: Standard media such as print, radio, and television were used in promoting this program.

Sponsor: At mid-season last year, Big O Tires stepped in as sponsor of "Ladies Night" and the Ladies Fan Club. Their tremendous help in paying for the jerseys this season allowed the Rockies to give the members even more value for their dollars. To activate their sponsorship, Big O gave out bounce-back coupons and premiums such as tire gauges to members.

Results: While first year results proved to be very successful, the numbers for the following quickly surpassed them. The program averaged about 1,300 fans each game, bringing the total season numbers to 15,600 participants. Because of the success of the ladies fan club, the Rockies started a parallel Guys Night Out program this season that resulted in great numbers in its first year with 1,100 participants per game.

Looking Ahead: The Rockies intend to keep moving forward with their promotions. This program uncovered a fan base of incredibly enthusiastic women who know baseball and love the Rockies. Using this promotion as a template, the club created the aforementioned "Guys Night Out" promotion that is yielding strong results. They also intend to apply the fan package concept to other markets as it has proven to be a powerful promotion tool.

Recommended Additional Readings

Irwin, R., Sutton, W., & McCarthy, L. (2008). *Sport promotion and sales management* (2nd ed.). Champaign, IL: Human Kinetics.

Veeck, M., & Williams, P. (2005). *Fun is good*. Emmaus, PA: Rodale. rodalestore.com.

The worksheets provide a guide for developing various sections of a marketing plan. The following sheets cover the marketing mix including product, price, place, promotion, marketing mix interactions, control and evaluation, and organizational structure and responsibilities specific to a marketing plan. Complete these worksheets as a preparatory step in the creation of a marketing plan.

Marketing Mix Worksheets

Detailed description of the products/services to be considered by the sport business.

_____

_____

_____

_____
_____
_____
_____
_____
_____
_____
_____

Calculate the price(s) that you will establish for your product(s) and service(s).

_____
_____
_____
_____
_____
_____
_____
_____
_____
_____

Delineate the place and distribution channels for your products and services.

_____
_____
_____
_____
_____
_____
_____
_____
_____
_____

Describe the promotional activities that will be implemented in your marketing plan.

_____
_____
_____
_____
_____
_____
_____
_____

Review the interactions between marketing mix variables.

_____

_____

_____

_____

_____

_____

_____

_____

_____

_____

_____

Chapter Eight

IMPLEMENTATION, CONTROL, AND EVALUATION

Implementation

The implementation of the marketing plan, like its planning, requires a team effort. No one person can get the marketing plan moving without synchronized activity across the organization. One of the best methods for implementing any project is the establishment of a project calendar. Although the scope of this workbook precludes an extensive discussion of project planning, a general format for the development of a project calendar may prove helpful. For a more detailed examination of these methods, the reader is encouraged to seek information from the variety of management texts in the field. The most popular systems are various critical path methodologies, such as Microsoft Project, Harvard Project Review, or Project Evaluation and Review Techniques (PERT), each of which is available in print versions or as integrated software programs.

The basic process for instigating an implementation calendar for a marketing plan is described below:

1. Identify all of the tasks required within the marketing plan.

2. Establish the sequence in which those tasks must be accomplished.

3. Estimate the amount of time necessary for the completion of each task individually.

4. Build a calendar (sometimes called a Gantt chart), which synthesizes the tasks and places them in their designated sequence, yet allows for the concurrent scheduling of tasks that can be performed simultaneously.

The implementation of any business activity also depends on the allocation of resources. When the marketing objectives were established, specific individuals within the organization were assigned tasks. This represented the allocation of human resources. The distribution of financial resources in the form of a marketing budget is also required for implementation. Stevens, Loudon, Wrenn, and Warren (1997) indicated that three bases for budget allocation are most common. First, financial resources can be distributed on a "percentage of sales" approach. This requires that a fixed percentage of either predicted or actual sales be set aside for marketing activities. The advantages of this approach are easy calculation and administration. However, because of variance in marketing different products in diverse markets, the "set percentage" may not be appropriate because it does not account for these variations. In addition, this approach continues an antiquated notion that sales levels should affect marketing allocations, as opposed to the contemporary concept, wherein marketing expenditures should influence sales.

The antithesis of the above approach is the "all-you-can-afford" approach (Stevens et al., 1997). Some organizations are so aggressive in their marketing activities that they will tax all available capital to get their product known to the market. All too often, more marketing activity is not the answer. Rather, a more targeted approach may be more effective. For most sport-related products, the days of mass marketing are over.

Finally, a more balanced approach to budget allocation resides in the "task or objective" approach. This method follows a well-established business practice of allocating resources directly to stated objectives. Just as you were asked to designate a person to be accountable for the accomplishment of each objective, a specific dollar figure can be matched to individual objectives. Stevens et al. (1997) supported this approach as having the most merit.

Control

Nothing stays on course forever. Through a marketing information system, a marketer can receive continuous feedback on consumer and market reactions to the marketing mix. The control mechanism should consist of top managers, including a marketing director or the group of decision-makers the organization charged with the task. Control should have, as its main function, the fine-tuning of the marketing plan in response to significant changes in the market or the industry. Constant tinkering (pulling up the plants to see if the roots are growing) can seriously hinder the marketing process and make control and evaluation efforts more difficult.

Stevens et al. (1997, p. 294) developed several questions that should be addressed in setting up the control functions for your marketing plan:

1. What kinds of data are needed to evaluate success?
2. Who will be responsible for collecting the data?
3. What time periods do you want to use to as checkpoints?
4. Who will conduct the analysis?
5. Who will receive the final reports?

Evaluation

The issue with evaluation is what to evaluate and when to do so. Sound management techniques lead back to the origin of the marketing process. Specific objectives were set, assigned to individuals in the organization, and targeted for accomplishment according to an established time line. Individual and Strategic Business Unit (SBU) accountability should be the focus of control efforts. Cohen (1998) suggests that all aspects of the marketing plan must be monitored on a periodic basis. Most management experts would agree that waiting until the end of the fiscal year to assess progress toward stated objectives would be ill advised. Too much can go wrong with even the best of marketing plans to wait until "judgment day" for assessment. Therefore, regular monitoring of progress is essential. On the other extreme, you don't want to burden managers with monthly reports addressing activities that may take several months to implement and assess. Therefore, perhaps the best interval for examining accomplishment is on a quarterly timeframe. This allows individuals to infuse their selected strategy, obtain authentic feedback on results, and work within changing parameters to meet their objectives.

Top management should also examine the over-all plan, SBU objectives, chosen strategy(s), and each element in the marketing mix. These are the criteria that should be used in the evaluation process.

Implementation, Control, and Evaluation Worksheets

The worksheets provide a guide for developing various sections of a marketing plan. The following sheets cover implementation, evaluation, and control mechanisms. Complete these worksheets as the final preparatory step in the creation of a marketing plan

Define the organizational structure and responsibilities that pertain to your marketing plan.

_____

_____

_____

_____

_____

_____

_____

_____

Develop an implementation calendar listing all of the tasks needed for implementation of your marketing plan.

_____

_____

_____

_____

_____

_____

_____

_____

_____

_____

_____

_____

List specific control criteria for implementation of your marketing plan.

_____
_____
_____
_____
_____
_____
_____
_____
_____
_____
_____
_____

Present a detailed description of resources allocated for the implementation phases of your marketing plan.

_____
_____
_____
_____
_____
_____
_____
_____
_____
_____
_____
_____

Specify the evaluation criteria and scheduled dates for formal evaluation of your marketing plan.

_____
_____
_____
_____
_____
_____
_____
_____

_____

_____

_____

_____

_____

Establish the means by which you will control and evaluate your marketing plan.

_____

_____

_____

_____

_____

_____

_____

_____

_____

References

Adams, R. (2004, March 2–April 4). MLB goes 2-for-2 in web distribution. *Sports Business Journal,* 5.

Armstrong, K. L. (1998). Ten strategies to employ when marketing sport to black consumers. *Sport Marketing Quarterly, 7*(3), 11–18.

Armstrong, K. L. (2004). Market analysis of race and sport consumption. *Sport Marketing Quarterly, 13*(1), 7–16.

Arnott, D. (1998, August 17–23). How do you sell what you can't see? *Sport Business Journal,* 39.

Associated Press (1991, August 30). Sports Business. *Associated Press wire service,* Slug/9120 3114.

Bagot, B. (1990, June). Shoe boom. *Marketing media decisions,* 61–66.

Bee, C. C., & Kahle, L. R. (2006). Relationship marketing in sports: A functional analysis. *Sport Marketing Quarterly, 15*(2), 102–110.

Boyd, T., & Kregbiel, T. (2003). Promotion timing in Major League Baseball and the stacking effects of factors that increase game attractiveness. *Sport Marketing Quarterly, 12*(3), 173–183.

Boyer, C. (2003). Survey says. *Athletic Administration, 38*(3), 48.

Brand management: Not just for sponsors anymore (2004, May 31). *IEG Sponsorship Report, 23*(10), 1, 4.

Brenner, S. (2004, May 31–June 6). A world of opportunity. *Sports Business Journal,* 15–16.

Brockinton, L. (1999, November 22–28). NBA deals open international markets. *Sports Business Journal,* 3.

Brooks, C. (1990, January). New aerobics markets. *Fitness Management,* 28–31.

Browes, R. (1998, October/November). When the going gets tough. *Australian Leisure Management,* 40–43.

Brown, G. (2003, March 31). A balanced brand. *NCAA News,* 3.

Brown, M. (2003). An analysis of online marketing in the sport industry. *Sport Marketing Quarterly, 12*(1), 48–55.

Bruce, K. (2004). Team as brand. Retrieved February 3, 2004, from http://migaliareport.com/feb04_story6.cfm

Burke, B. (2003, September 22–28). Sponsorship report card: Athletic shoes and apparel. *Sports Business Journal,* 26.

Chen, C. Y., Stotlar, D. K., & Lin, Y. H. (2007). *Data mining in professional sports using multinomial prohibit model sponsorship.* Denver, CO: Western Decision Science Institute.

Christie, L. (2004). *The selling of the tournament.* Retrieved June 21, 2004, from http://money.cnn.com/2004/06/17/news/usopen prices/index.htm.

Coffey, B. (2002, December 23). Retail redemption. *Forbes,* 372–373.

Cohen, A. (1995, January). Gray areas. *Athletic Business,* 31–40.

Cohen, W. A. (1998). *Marketing planning guide* (2nd ed.). New York: Wiley.

Cole, P. E. (1988, March 14). Sweat meets glitz at the L.A. Marathon. *Business Week,* 38.

Cova, B., & Cova, V. (2004). *Tribal marketing: The tribalization of society and its impact on the conduct of marketing.* Retrieved June 19, 2004, from http://visionarymarketing.com. The paper can also be found in the special issue of the *European Journal of Marketing 2002, 36*(5), 595.

Crawford, D. (1998, August 31–September 6). Bigger, lighter rackets not without critics. *Sports Business Journal,* 23.

Eby, S. M. (1987). Psssst! (Do you want to know a secret?). Small Business Success. Boston: Inc. Publishing Company.

Erch, F. R. (1998, September). Brand image, positioning and service quality. *European Journal for Sport Marketing,* 82–105.

Fan promotions: An important part of the sport experience (1998, October 26–November 1). *Sport Business Journal,* 23–26.

Farris, P. W., Bendle, N. T., Pfeifer, P. E., & Reibstein, D. J. (2006). *Marketing metrics: 50+ metrics every executive should master.* Upper Saddle River, NJ: Wharton School Publishing.

Ferraro, C. (1994, February 22). Colorado scaling new heights. *Rocky Mountain News,* 30A.

Fielitz, L., & Scott, D. (2003). Prediction of physical performance using data mining. *Research Quarterly for Exercise and Sport, 74*(1), 25.

Fullerton, S. (2007). *Sports marketing.* New York: McGraw-Hill.

Gray, D. P. (1991). Sport marketing. In B. Parkhouse (Ed.), *The management of sport.* St. Louis: Mosby Times Mirror.

Greenspan, R. (2003). *Sports content revenue soars, scores.* Retrieved December 14, 2003, from http://www.clickz.com/stats/markets/ broadband/article.php/10099_214511

Grey, A. M., & Skildum-Reid, K. (2007). *The sponsorship seekers toolkit* (2nd ed.). Sydney: McGraw-Hill.

Grönroos, C. (1994, August). From marketing mix to relationship marketing: Towards a paradigm shift in marketing. *Asia-Australia Marketing Journal, 2*(1), 9–30.

Hamel, G. (1998, December 7). The e-corporation. *Fortune,* 82–92.

Handel, C. (1997, Spring). Database marketing: Increasing participation in recreational sport. *NIRSA Journal,* 46–48.

Haner, N. (2004, May 3–9). Giants fans high on Wi-Fi after installation at SBC Park. *Sport Business Journal,* 9.

Hemingway, P. (2002, August 23). Sports waking up to growing Latino market. *Central New York Business Journal,* 11, 15.

Hiebing, R. G., & Cooper, S. W. (2003). *The successful marketing plan.* New York: McGraw-Hill.

Hightower, R., Brady, M., & Baker, T. (2002). Investigating the role of the physical environment in hedonic service consumption: An exploratory study of sporting events. *Journal of Business Research, 55,* 697–707.

Hill, R., Pine, B., Gilmore, J., Betts, P., Houmann, L., & Stubblefield, A. (2001). Welcome to the experience economy. *Health Forum Journal, 44*(5), 44–53.

Internet Advertising Bureau (2003). *IAB/PWC report $1.66 billion internet ad revenue for Q3 2003.* Retrieved November 29, 2003, from http://www.iab.net/news/pr_2003_11_11.asp.

James, J., & Ross, S. (2004). Comparing sport consumer motivations across multiple sports. *Sport Marketing Quarterly, 13*(1), 7–16.

Jones, V. N. (1989, February 12). Morgan Turner. *Rocky Mountain News,* p. D4.

Kaplan, D. (1998, September 21–27). Rawlings takes a hit over new NCAA bat rule. *Sports Business Journal,* 14.

Kenneth, P. A., Sneath, J. Z., & Erdmann, J. W. (1997, summer). Using demographics to segment your market. *International Sports Journal, 1*(1), 54–62.

Kim, G. (2004, March). *Three out of four Americans have access to the internet.* Retrieved November 15, 2004, from http://www.neilsen-netratings.com/pr/pr_040318.pdf.

Kim, C., & Mauborgne, R. (2004, October). Blue ocean strategy. *Harvard Business Review,* 76–84.

Kim, S. J., & Stotlar, D. K. (2007) *Profiling golfers on the basis of innovativeness.* Ft. Lauderdale, FL: North American Society for Sport Management.

King, B. (2002, December). Passion that can't be counted puts billions of dollars into play. *Sport Business Journal, 4,* 25–39.

Kotler, P. (1992). It's time for total marketing. *Business Week ADVANCE Executive Brief,* Vol. 2.

Kotler, P. (1994). *Marketing management.* Englewood Cliffs, NJ: Prentice-Hall.

Kotler, P. (1997). Marketing management: Analysis, planning, implementation and control. Upper Saddle River, NJ: Prentice Hall.

Kotler, P. (2003). *Marketing insights from A to Z.* Hoboken, NJ: John Wiley & Sons.

Kotler, P., & Andreasen, A. R. (1987). *Strategic marketing for nonprofit organizations* (3rd ed.). Englewood Cliffs, NJ: Prentice-Hall Inc.

Kotler, P., & Armstrong, G. (2006). *Principles of marketing* (11th ed.). Upper Saddle River, NJ: Prentice Hall.

Kotler, P., & Cox, K. (1980). *Marketing management and strategy.* Englewood Cliffs, N.J.: Prentice-Hall Inc.

Kovatch, K. (1998, November 9–15). Once an outsider, ski maker K2 finds a home, respect. *Sports Business Journal,* 21.

Kwon, H. H., & Armstrong, K. L. (2004). An exploration of the construct of psychological attachment to a sport team among college students: A multidimensional approach. *Sport Marketing Quarterly, 13*(2), 82–93.

Lackett, K. (2003, September 14). Getting down to specifics. *Ft. Collins Coloradoan,* G1-2.

Lake, M. (2004). Silver secret behind golden hopes. Retrieved July 21, 2004, from http://www.cnn.com/2004/TECH/07/20/noble.fibers/index.html

Laster, J. (2004). The team dealer. Retrieved July 8, 2004, from http://www.sgma.com/sportsedge/articles/2004/7/article10909 62571-26376.shtml

Lauer, H. (2006). *The new Americans.* Cortland Manor, NY: American Sports Data.

Lee, J. (2003, November 3–9). DaimlerChrysler deal packages 3 conferences 32 black colleges. *Sports Business Journal,* 18.

Levine, J. (1993, December, 20). Relationship marketing. *Forbes, 152*(14), 232–234.

Lidz, F., Kenndey, K., & Deitch, R. (2002, November 25). Promo sapiens. *Sports Illustrated, 97*(21), 25.

McCarthy, E. J., & Perreault, W. D. (1990). *Basic marketing* (10th ed.). Boston: Irwin.

McCarthy, L. M., & Stillman, W. P. (1998). Marketing to Hispanic consumers. *Sport Marketing Quarterly, 7*(4), 19–24.

McConnell, B., & Huba, J. (2004). *Creating customer evangelists: How loyal fans can become a volunteer sales force.* Retrieved July 2, 2004, from http//:www.mialiareport.com/jul04_story5.cfm

McDonald, M., & Keegan, W. (2003). *Marketing plans that work.* Boston: Butterworth Heinemann.

McDonald, M., & Sutton, W. (1995). TEAMQUAL (TM): Measuring service quality in professional team sports. *Sport Marketing Quarterly, 4*(2), 15–26.

Meek, A. (1997). An estimate of the size and supported economic activity of the sports industry in the United States. *Sport Marketing Quarterly, 6*(4), 15–21.

Migala, D. (2003). My buddies: Heat and Suns use internal marketing program to improve relations with season ticket holders. *The Migala Report.* Retrieved December 2, 2003, from http://www.migaliareport.com/dec03_story4.cfm

Migala, D. (2005, May 1). Collection house: Effective strategies to collect email addresses for future ticket mailings. *The Migala Report.*

Miller, E. (1998, January 27). Surviving skier suffers frostbite. *Denver Post,* 2D.

Miller, J., & Veltri, F. (2004). *Consumer purchasing behavior of sport merchandise/apparel online.* North American Society for Sport Management Annual Conference, Atlanta.

Miller L. K., & Fielding, L. W. (1997). Ticket distribution agencies and professional sport franchises: The successful partnership. *Sports Marketing Quarterly, 6*(1), 47–60.

Miller, L., Shaad, S., Burch, D., & Turner, R. (1999). *Sales success in sport marketing.* Wichita, KS: Events Unlimited

Milner, C. (2003, March). Same old story? *Athletic Business,* 59–64.

Moore, P. (1998, July 6–12). Marketing by the numbers. *Sports Business Journal,* 12.

Morrell, J. (2004, July). Seat of learning. *Stadia Magazine, 29,* 42–44.

Most effective MLB promotions (2003, October 20–36). *Sport Business Journal,* 43.

Mullen, L. (1998, June 29–July, 5). Univision scoring big with World Cup games. *Sport Business Journal,* 4.

Mullin, B. (1985). Internal marketing in successful sport management. In G. Lewis & H. Appenzeller (Eds.) *Successful sport management* (pp. 157–175). Charlottesville, VA: Michie Company.

Mullin, B., Hardy, S., & Sutton W. A. (2007). *Sport marketing* (3rd ed.). Champaign, IL: Human Kinetics.

Myerson, A. R. (1996, May 31). Olympic sponsors battling to defend turf. *New York Times,* D1, D17.

National Basketball Association, (1998). *NBA international facts.* New York: National Basketball Association.

Nielsen Media. (2004, November 30). *How American shops.* Provided by Nielsen Marketing, a division of VNU USA. http://vnu.usa.com.

Pallerino, M. (2004, July). You paid what for that? *Sports Edge, 4*(7), 4.

Parker, P. (1998, February 1). Resorts catering to over-50 ski crowd. *Denver Post,* p. 1L.

Pebble Beach v. Tour 18, (942 F. Supp 1513).

Pitts, B., & Fielding, L. (1989). *Implementing a total system concept of marketing: Hillerich and Bradsby 1915–1923.* Presentation at the 4th annual Conference of the North American Society for Sport Management. Calgary, Alberta.

Pitts B. G., & Stotlar, D. K. (2002). *Fundamentals of sport marketing* (2nd ed.). Morgantown, WV: Fitness Information Technology.

Pitts B. G., & Stotlar, D. K. (2007). *Fundamentals of sport marketing* (3rd ed.). Morgantown, WV: Fitness Information Technology.

Plunkett Research (2007). *US Sports Industry Overview.* Retrieved December 17, 2007, from http://www.plunkettresaerch.com/Industries/Sports/SportsStatistics.aspx

Pollard, A. G. (1997, May). Measure for measure: Sizing up the new golf clubs. *Hemisphere,* 47–50.

Pride, W. M., & Ferrell, O. C. (2008). *Marketing* (14th ed.). New York: Houghton Mifflin Company.

Reese, J., & Mittlestadt, R. (2001). An exploratory study of the criteria used to establish NFL ticket prices. *Sport Marketing Quarterly, 10*(4), 223–230.

Ries, A., & Trout, J. (1986). *Positioning: The battle for your mind.* New York: McGraw-Hill.

Roberts, K. (1997, July). Proof that image really is everything. *Sport Business, 12,* 22–23.

Rodin, S. (1998, May 11–17). Shrewd marketers can share in boom. *Sport Business Journal,* 34.

Rofé, J. (1998, August 31–September 6). Equipment sales going to the dogs. *Sports Business Journal,* 22.

Rofé, J. (1998, November 9–15). An extremely profitable niche. *Sport Business Journal,* 28.

Rohm, A. (1997). The creation of consumer bonds with Reebok running. *Sport Marketing Quarterly, 6*(2), 17–25.

Rudolph, B. (1989, Aug. 28). Foot's paradise. *Time,* 54–55.

Salerno, S. (1991, March). Baseball bonanza. *American West Magazine,* 43–49.

S&MM (2004, August 15). New York: Sales & Marketing Management, Inc.

SGMA (2004). Sports apparel & athletic footwear—U.S. market facts/trends. Retrieved July 27, 2004, from http://www.sgma.com/reports/2004/report1090951630-31665.html

SGMA (2006). *Finding: Sports gear, clothing & shoe sales near $60 Billion.* Retrieved December 20, 2007, from http://www.sgma.com/displayindustryarticle.cfm?articlenbr=31286&startrec=51

SGMA (2007). *Sports participation in the USA—A national attraction.* North Palm Beach FL: Sporting Goods Manufactures Association. Retrieved December 19, 2007, from http://www.sgma.com/displayindustryarticle.cfm?articlenbr=34693

Shanahan, M. (1999). *Think like a champion: Building success one victory at a time.* New York: Harper Collins.

Shani, D., & Chalasani, S. (1992). Exploring niches using relationship marketing. *Journal of Consumer Marketing, 9*(3), 33–42.

Shelley, L. (2004). *Demographics and dividends.* Retrieved March 3, 2004, from http://clubindustry.com.news.fintess-demographics-dividends/

Skildum-Reid, K. (2007). *The ambush marketing toolkit.* North Ryde, NSW: McGraw-Hill.

Smart money. (1998, December). Retrieved January 7, 1999, from http://www.smartmeoney.com

Spoelstra, J. (1997). *Ice to the Eskimos: How to sell a product nobody wants.* New York: Harper Business.

Steinbach, P. (2002, December). Value judgments. *Athletic Business,* 22–24.

Stern, W. (1993, May 24). Buy me some arepa and media noche. *Forbes,* 184.

Stevens, R. E., Loudon, D. L., Wrenn, B., & Warren, W. E. (1997). *Market planning guide.* New York: Haworth Press.

Stotlar D. K., & Johnson, D. A. (1989). Assessing the impact and effectiveness of stadium advertising on sport spectators at division one institutions. *Journal of Sport Management, 3*(2), 90–102.

Stoufer, D. (1998, November 9–15). X faithful may be young, but they're smart and savvy about their sports. *Sport Business Journal,* 29.

Sutton, W. A. (1996, June). 76ers community intercept surveys suggest new marketing tactics. *Team Marketing Report,* 7.

Torsiello, J. (1998, July 27–August 2). Tough to swing in club scene. *Sports Business Journal, 1,* 16.

VanAuken, B. (2002). *The brand management checklist.* London: Kogan Page Limited.

Williams, P. (1998, June 1–7). Firm's cyber-seats offer interactive experience of pro sports events. *Sports Business Journal,* 15.

Zabib, J., & Brebach, G. (2004). *Precision marketing.* Hoboken, NJ; Wiley & Sons, Inc.

Zavian, E. (1998, July 20–26). Entrepreneurs saw shapes of things to come in women's clothing. *Sports Business Journal,* 27.

Zhang, Z., & Won, D. (2004). *Trust and consumption of licensed sport merchandise on the Internet.* North American Society for Sport Management, 2004 Conference, Atlanta, GA.

Index

About the Author

Dr. David K. Stotlar teaches on the University of Northern Colorado faculty in the areas of sport marketing, sponsorship, and event management. He has had more than 60 articles published in professional journals and has written several textbooks and book chapters on sport management and marketing. He has made numerous presentations at international and national professional conferences. On several occasions, he has served as a consultant in sport management to various sport professionals and in the area of sport marketing and sponsorship, to multinational corporations and international sport managers. Dr. Stotlar was selected by the United States Olympic Committee as a delegate to the International Olympic Academy in Greece and the World University Games Forum in Italy and served as a venue media center supervisor for the 2002 Olympic Games. He has conducted international seminars in sport management and marketing for the Hong Kong Olympic Committee, the National Sports Council of Malaysia, Mauritius National Sports Council, the National Sports Council of Zimbabwe, the Singapore Sports Council, the Chinese Taipei University Sport Federation, the Bahrain Sport Institute, the government of Saudi Arabia, the South African National Sports Congress, and the Association of Sport Sciences in South Africa. Dr. Stotlar's contribution to the profession includes an appointment as Coordinator of the Sport Management Program Review Council (NASPE/NASSM) from 1999–2001. He previously served as Chair of the Council on Facilities and Equipment of the American Alliance for Health, Physical Education, Recreation and Dance and as a Board Member and later as President of the North American Society for Sport Management. Dr. Stotlar was a member of the initial group of professionals inducted as NASSM Research Fellows. He is also a founding member of the Sport Marketing Association.